Canning
Freezing & Drying

By the Editors of Sunset Books
and Sunset Magazine

Lane Publishing Co., Menlo Park, California

Edited by Linda Brandt

Special Consultants:

Dr. George K. York
Food Technologist
University of California at Davis

Paulette DeJong
Staff Research Associate
University of California at Davis

Jean E. Lebbert
Staff Editor, Sunset Magazine

Design: **Cynthia Hanson**

Photography: **Darrow M. Watt**

Photo Editor: **Lynne B. Morrall**

Illustrations: **Nancy Lawton**

Cover: Summer's bounty of fresh fruits and vegetables—beautiful candidates for canning, freezing, and drying. Photographed by Darrow M. Watt.

First Printing April 1981
Editor, Sunset Books: David E. Clark

CONTENTS

CANNING

Ascorbic acid: packaged, white crystalline form of vitamin C used to prevent discoloration of fruit and vegetables.

Boiling-water method: see Water bath method.

Botulism: a deadly form of food spoilage that can occur when low-acid vegetables, meat, poultry, and seafood are canned incorrectly or by method other than the steam pressure method.

Cold pack (or "raw pack"): clean, unheated jars are filled with cold, uncooked food before processing. Often used when preparing soft-textured foods that need to be packed carefully.

Hot pack: hot jars are filled with hot, precooked food before processing. Used when preparing firm-textured foods because it allows tighter packing in jars.

Jell point: temperature or cooking point at which jelly slides off a spoon in a sheet. Jelly reaches its jell point at a temperature 8°F (4°C) higher than the boiling point of water.

Pickling: method of preserving any food in brine or vinegar. This includes vegetables, fruit, relishes, and chutney.

Processing: canning jars of food by a method that destroys harmful molds, bacteria, and enzymes.

Steam pressure method: canning method used for processing jars of vegetables, meat, poultry, and seafood. Steam in canner is under enough pressure to reach high temperatures (240°F /116°C), thus destroying bacteria and sterilizing contents of jars.

Venting: allowing excess air inside a pressure canner to escape through vent before closing the petcock or putting on the weighted gauge.

Water bath method: canning method used for processing jars of food high in acid, such as fruit and tomatoes. High temperature in kettle provides enough heat through jars to sterilize contents.

What happens in canning?

There's no special magic to canning. Fruits, vegetables, or meats are packed into canning jars, which are fitted with self-sealing lids and then heated. Sustained high heat kills dangerous organisms that could cause food spoilage in the jars; it also causes the gases in the food and in the jars to expand, driving out most of the air left inside. Hot jams, jellies, and other preserves are cooked first and then packed, hot, into hot jars.

When a jar cools, the vacuum created inside pulls the lid down against the jar mouth to make a tight seal. Unless the seal is broken, none of the organisms that cause spoilage can enter.

Equipment you'll need

It's very important to use the right equipment when you can; everything from the canning jars to the right kettle is crucial. If you're a beginner and are starting out with nothing, consider sharing equipment expenses with a friend. You can take turns canning or—better still—can together.

Canning jars, made of tempered glass that can withstand heat shock and rough treatment, are recommended. Easily recognized by the manufacturer's name or a pattern blown into the glass, they can be purchased in most grocery stores or housewares departments in half-pint, pint, and quart sizes.

Parts of a Canning Jar

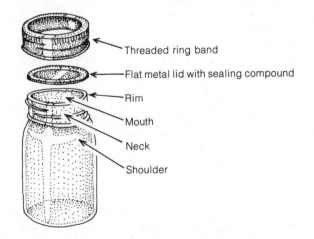

- Threaded ring band
- Flat metal lid with sealing compound
- Rim
- Mouth
- Neck
- Shoulder

Canning jars come in different shapes. The wide-mouthed ones are most convenient for packing large pieces of food such as pickles or chunks of meat. Small jars are good for jams, jellies, or individual servings. Special fancy jars with brightly colored lids are available just for jelly-making.

Old-fashioned canning jars—called *lightning jars*—have glass lids that clamp down over rubber rings; these jars can be used if they are made of tempered glass (those sold in gift shops usually are not) and have double (not single) wire clamps.

To use a lightning jar, fit a wet rubber ring to the little sealing ledge on the neck of the filled jar. Put on the glass lid so it rests on the rubber ring. Grasp the longest of the two wire clamps (bails), pulling it up to a little groove in the lid. Let the shorter wire hang down while the food is being processed; then immediately clamp the shorter wire down to seal the jar when you take it out of the canner. Lightning jars have two drawbacks—1) the rubber rings usually are not reusable and replacements may be difficult to find; and 2) when the jars have been processed, it's hard to tell if they're sealed.

Another old-fashioned type of jar has a zinc cap with a porcelain lining and rubber ring. These caps can be reused if in good condition. To use them, fit a new rubber ring down to the sealing ledge of an empty jar—don't stretch the ring unnecessarily. Pack the jar, wipe the ring and jar rim clean, and screw the cap down firmly. Then unscrew it ¼ inch—this will allow air in the jar to vent properly. Immediately after processing, screw the cap down tightly to complete the seal. Once cooled, tilt the jar to see if it leaks; if so, the jar isn't sealed.

A canning kettle is needed to process acid foods, such as fruit, tomatoes, and some pickles. Any kettle large enough for the jars to be completely immersed and fully surrounded by hot water is acceptable. You can improvise with a large stock pot and cover, using a cake rack in the bottom to rest jars on, but a kettle especially made for the purpose is much easier to use. Canning kettles (see photo on page 18) come with a metal basket to separate and hold the jars off the bottom of the kettle so that heat can circulate properly and filled jars can be lowered and raised simply.

A steam canner, recently reintroduced on the market, is an alternative to a canning kettle for processing acid foods such as fruit. (It cannot be used to replace a steam pressure canner—see next page.)

Resembling an inverted kettle, it has a shallow panlike bottom fitted with a tray. Jars of fruit rest on the tray, and a tall, tight-fitting cover fits on top. This type of canner does not shorten the processing time. However, since a smaller amount of water is used than in a canning kettle, the steam canner heats to a boil more quickly. This will reduce your overall canning time.

Our research suggests that pickles are more satisfactory when processed in a regular canning kettle, because water temperatures can be regulated better.

A steam pressure canner is a heavy kettle with a cover that locks down to become steamtight. Mounted on the cover are a safety valve, petcock vent, and a pressure indicator. The pressure indicator will be one of two types: a weighted gauge or a dial gauge.

The weighted gauge automatically limits pressure by a control preset for 5, 10, or 15 pounds. The dial-shaped gauge has a needle that indicates pressure on a numbered face.

Whichever type you select, remember that a steam pressure canner is the *only* home-canning device that can apply enough high heat to ensure the safe canning of low-acid foods—vegetables, meat, poultry, and fish.

It's important that your steam pressure canner be in good working order. Check the pressure dial gauge for accuracy each season before using the canner, either with the manufacturer or, in some states, with the county cooperative extension service. Thread a piece of string through the petcock and safety valve openings to make sure they are free of obstruction. Follow the manufacturer's directions for using your particular steam pressure canner, and follow exactly the directions in this book for the specific food you're canning.

Helpful accessories include a colander for scalding (blanching) fruits and vegetables, long-handled spoons and ladles, a food processor or food chopper for grinding up foods, a wide-

mouthed funnel for easy filling of jars, a jar lifter or rubber-tipped tongs for handling hot jars, an accurate thermometer to check temperatures, measuring cups and spoons, and an accurate scale. A few other items with more specific uses appear in the photograph on page 18.

Method of canning

Safety is crucial in canning. In general, there are two basic methods of canning—the *water bath method* and the *steam pressure method*. Later in this chapter, detailed step-by-step canning directions will be given for fruit, vegetables, meat, and fish, as well as for jam, jelly, and pickles.

The water bath method can be used safely with fruit, tomatoes, and pickles. Jars full of these acid foods are heated in a hot water bath, using the canning kettle or steam canner described on page 5. The simmering hot (180° to 190°F) water provides enough heat to destroy the organisms that might cause spoilage in these foods.

The steam pressure method *must* be used when canning all other vegetables (low-acid vegetables), meat, poultry, and fish. All of these foods are processed in jars under high pressure in the steam pressure canner described at left.

What about the dangers of canning?

Nearly everyone has heard about a deadly form of food poisoning called *botulism*. It's a type of food spoilage that usually occurs in low-acid foods. The organisms that cause it have some peculiar characteristics: they thrive without air in sealed jars, can't be destroyed by being processed at the temperature of boiling water (212°F) in a reasonable amount of time, and can't be easily detected when a jar is opened.

Though botulism doesn't occur in acid foods such as tomatoes and other fruits, it can occur in virtually all vegetables, meat, poultry, and fish. That is why these foods must *always* be processed at 240°F in the steam pressure canner. Before canning any type of food, read "Guard Against Botulism" on page 37.

Other types of food spoilage that might occur if jars of food aren't sealed properly are more easily detected. If the food smells bad or is soft, discolored, or moldy, discard it without tasting it. When in doubt, throw it out!

CANNING FRESH FRUITS

Fresh fruit and tomatoes can be canned confidently using the water bath method described at left. You just fill hot canning jars with fruit, cover with a liquid, top them with lids and ring bands, place them in a canning kettle of simmering water, and heat them for a specified length of time. There are two ways of packing fruit.

Cold pack or raw pack involves putting cut raw fruit right into the jars and then pouring hot syrup over it to within ½ inch of the jar rim. This method is good for most small or soft fruits, such as apricots.

Hot pack involves cooking the fruit briefly in syrup, packing the hot fruit into hot jars, and then pouring hot syrup over the fruit to within ½ inch of the jar rim. This method is best for large fruit pieces, such as peach or pear halves. They usually shrink in cooking and become more pliable, so you can fit more into each jar.

Protecting fruit colors

Some fruits have a tendency to darken when cut and must be treated to retain their bright colors. The chart on pages 10 and 11 indicates which ones need to be treated.

An easy way to prevent darkening is to slice the fruit directly into a solution of 2 tablespoons *each* salt and vinegar and 1 gallon of water.

Or you can use a commercial antidarkening agent (antioxidant—available at most supermarkets) or a powdered form of ascorbic acid (vitamin C—available at most drugstores), mixing 3 tablespoons powder into 2 quarts water. You don't need to rinse off the solution before placing fruit in jars.

Is sugar necessary?

It's fine to can without adding sugar, but some sweetening improves the flavor as well as the appearance of most fruit; it also keeps fruit firmer and helps prevent them from floating in the jars. You have to pour a liquid of some kind over the fruit when the jars are packed; it can be a syrup made of water mixed with sugar or honey (or some of each), a sweetened or unsweetened fruit juice (such as unsweetened pineapple juice or white grape juice), or just water. You can also make juice by crushing soft fruit, heating it, and then straining it.

The following table gives recommended proportions of sweetener to water, and the syrup yield of each. All the syrups have good flavor and texture, but those with the highest proportions of sugar will usually make the most attractive product.

SYRUP RECIPES	YIELD
Light syrup	
2 cups sugar, 4 cups water	5 cups syrup
1 cup honey, 1 cup sugar, 4 cups water	5½ cups syrup
1 cup honey, 3 cups water	4 cups syrup
Medium syrup	
3 cups sugar, 4 cups water	5½ cups syrup
1 cup honey, 2 cups sugar, 4 cups water	6 cups syrup
2 cups honey, 2 cups water	4 cups syrup
Heavy syrup	
4¼ cups sugar, 4 cups water	6½ cups syrup

If you want to use honey, choose a mild-flavored one, such as clover. Don't use a higher proportion of honey than is suggested above—it will mask the flavor of the fruit. For the same reason, brown sugar, raw sugar, molasses, and sorghum should not be used.

You'll need 1 to 1½ cups syrup for each quart of fruit. Combine the sugar or honey with water in a pan and heat to a boil, stirring constantly until dissolved.

Step-by-step canning for fruits & tomatoes

1 Read the preceding information on canning fruit, and check the fruit chart (pages 10 and 11) for instructions on the particular fruit you're about to can. The chart will also tell you which fruits need to be treated to prevent darkening when cut (see "Protecting fruit colors," page 7).

2 Get out canning kettle, jars (discard any that have nicks or cracks), lids (they must be new), ring bands, and other items listed under "Equipment you'll need," page 5). Be sure all equipment is clean and ready to use. Scald lids in boiling water; keep in very hot water until time to use. If you plan to use the hot pack method, place jars in a kettle of very hot water until ready to use. Otherwise, jars just need to be clean.

Check jars for nicks or cracks

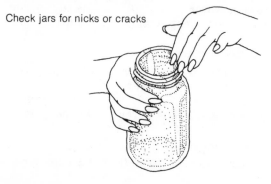

3 Place rack in canning kettle and fill kettle about half full with hot water. Place kettle, covered, on range element to heat. In a large teakettle or another pan, heat additional water to add later.

4 Following chart directions, prepare only enough fruit for one canner load at a time. Make syrup of your choice (see page 7). Heat syrup until sugar or honey is dissolved (or heat water or fruit juice); keep it hot (but not boiling) until ready to use.

Prepare only enough fruit for one canner load at a time

5 Fruit can be packed cold and raw or hot and precooked. Remove a jar from the hot water (if using hot pack method).

Pack fruit, cavity side down with pieces overlapping, into clean, hot jar

To pack fruits cold (except tomatoes), fill jars with raw fruit, cavity side down, with layers overlapping; then ladle hot syrup into clean, unheated jars, filling each to within ¼ inch of jar rim.

To pack food hot, bring syrup or other liquid to boiling in a large pan, add prepared fruit pieces, and cook briefly as directed. Remove fruit from syrup and pack into hot jars, cavity side down, with layers overlapping; then pour over enough of the syrup to fill jars to within ¼ inch of rims, or as directed in recipe.

Fill jar with syrup, leaving ¼-inch head space

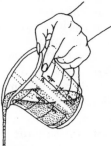

6 Run a narrow spatula gently around each jar between food and jar sides to release any bubbles; add more liquid, if necessary.

Release air bubbles before applying lid

7 Wipe jar rim with damp cloth to remove any food particles that might prevent a seal. Lift a jar lid from hot water and place it on jar (if lids stick together, plunge into cold water, then hot). Screw ring band on by hand; don't overtighten. Repeat with remaining jars. As each jar is filled, set it on rack in canning kettle. Arrange jars on rack so they aren't touching each other or sides of kettle.

8 When all jars are filled and set in canner, add enough boiling water from teakettle to

Add enough hot water to submerge jars at least ½ inch

submerge jars at least ½ inch under the surface. Cover canner and turn heat to high. As soon as water starts to break the surface at a hard simmer, reduce heat and simmer, covered or uncovered, for the time required for processing (see chart on pages 10 and 11).

9 Keep water at a gentle boil; a vigorous boil evaporates the water too fast and is unnecessary because temperatures reached at a hard simmer are sufficient for safe canning. If canning at altitudes above 3,000 feet, add 2 minutes processing time for each additional 1,000 feet. (If liquid is lost from jar during processing, don't open the jar and add more liquid unless you intend to process it again. Liquid loss will not cause spoilage.)

10 Remove jars with a jar lifter. (Do not cool in the canner or food will overcook.) Set jars on a folded cloth or board—never on a cold surface. Leave enough room between jars for air to circulate.

11 When jars are cool, remove ring bands, if desired. (To loosen a band that sticks, cover with a hot, damp cloth for 1 to 2 minutes; then loosen.) Test seal by pressing lid with your finger. If it stays down when pressed, the jar is sealed; if lid pops back up, it is not sealed.

Test seal by pressing lid with your finger; it should stay down

12 If a jar hasn't sealed by the time it's cool, refrigerate and use food within a few days—if it looks and smells all right.
   Wash sealed, cooled jars and rings in warm soapy water to remove excess syrup and prevent water spots; rinse and dry.

13 Label jars and store in a cool, dark place.

Guide for Canning Fruit

Note: At elevations higher than 3,000 feet, add 2 minutes processing time for each additional 1,000 feet.

Fruit	Quantity to yield 1 pint	How to prepare	Processing time Pints	Quarts
Apples Golden Delicious, Gravenstein, Jonathan, McIntosh, Yellow Newtown Pippin	1¼ to 1½ lbs.	Pare and remove cores; cut in slices or quarters; treat to prevent darkening. Cook in syrup or other liquid for 2 to 4 minutes; pack hot and cover with hot cooking liquid, leaving ¼" head space. Apply lid and ring band.	15 min.	15 min.
Apricots Blenheim (Royal), Tilton, Wenatchee	1 to 1¼ lbs.	Peel as for nectarines, if desired. Cut in half and remove pits, or leave whole; treat for darkening. _To pack hot_, cook whole apricots in syrup or other liquid for 1 to 3 minutes; pack hot; cover with hot cooking liquid, leaving ¼" head space. Apply lid and ring band. _To pack raw_, fill jar with whole or halved apricots; cover with hot syrup or other liquid, leaving ¼" head space. Apply lid and ring band.	20 min. 25 min.	20 min. 30 min.
Bananas		Canning not recommended.		
Berries (Except strawberries, which are not recommended for canning)	¾ to 1½ lbs.	_If berries are firm_, add about ½ cup sugar to 1 quart fruit in a pan; bring to boil, shaking pan to prevent sticking; pack hot; cover with hot syrup or other liquid, leaving ¼" head space. Apply lid and ring band. _If berries are soft_, fill jar with raw fruit; shake down; cover with hot syrup or berry juice, leaving ¼" head space. Apply lid and ring band.	10 min. 10 min.	10 min. 15 min.
Cherries, sweet Bing, Black Tartarian, Lambert, Royal Ann (Napoleon)	1 to 1½ lbs.	Pit, if desired; prick skins if left whole. _To pack hot_, bring cherries to a boil in syrup or other liquid; pack hot; cover with hot cooking liquid, leaving ¼" head space. Apply lid and ring band. _To pack raw_, pack fruit in jar; cover with boiling syrup or other liquid, leaving ¼" head space. Apply lid and ring band.	15 min. 20 min.	15 min. 25 min.
Figs Black Mission, Celeste, Kadota, Brown Turkey (Black Mission)	¾ to 1¼ lbs.	Bring to a boil in water or syrup; let stand 3 to 4 minutes. Pack hot; add 1½ teaspoons lemon juice per pint; cover with hot liquid or syrup, leaving ¼" head space. Apply lid and ring band.	90 min.	90 min.
Grapefruit	2 lbs.	Use thoroughly ripened fruit. Cut off peel, including white membrane; lift out segments and pack into jars. Cover with hot syrup or other liquid, leaving ¼" head space. Apply lid and ring band.	30 min.	35 min.
Grapes Use ripe Muscat or slightly underripe Thompson seedless grapes	2 lbs.	Remove stems. _To pack hot_, bring to a boil in a small amount of light or medium syrup or other liquid; pack hot; cover with hot syrup, leaving ¼" head space. Apply lid and ring band. _To pack raw_, put into jars and cover with hot syrup or other liquid, leaving ¼" head space. Apply lid and ring band.	15 min. 20 min.	15 min. 20 min.
Lemons and **limes**		Canning not recommended.		
Loquats	1½ to 2 lbs.	Remove stem and blossom ends; cut in half and remove seeds. Cook for 3 to 5 minutes in syrup or other liquid. Pack hot; cover with hot cooking liquid, leaving ¼" head space. Apply lid and ring band.	15 min.	20 min.
Melons		Canning not recommended.		

Fruit	Quantity to yield 1 pint	How to prepare	Processing time Pints	Quarts
Nectarines Flaming Globe, Freedom, Gold Mine, Gower, Late le Grand, Panamint, Stanwick	1 to 1½ lbs.	To peel (if desired) dip in boiling water, plunge in cold water, then pull off skins. (Pare unevenly ripened fruit). Cut along seam, twist in half, and remove pits. Treat to prevent darkening. *To pack hot,* heat in boiling syrup or other liquid until hot through; or, if fruit is juicy, add 1 cup sugar to 1 quart fruit and heat slowly just to boiling. Pack hot, then cover with hot syrup or cooking liquid, leaving ¼″ head space. Apply lid and ring band. *To pack raw,* place fruit, cut side down, in jar; cover with hot syrup or other liquid, leaving ¼″ head space. Apply lid and ring band.	(Freestone) 20 min. 25 min. (Clingstone) 25 min. 30 min.	
Oranges		Canning not recommended.		
Peaches Elberta, J. H. Hale, Redglobe, Redhaven, Rio Oso Gem, Veteran	1 to 1½ lbs.	Peel and can as directed for nectarines.	(Freestone) 15 min. 20 min. (Clingstone) 20 min. 20 min.	
Pears Bartlett	1 to 1½ lbs.	Pare, cut in half, and remove cores; treat for darkening. *To pack hot,* cook in boiling syrup or other liquid just until heated through; pack hot and cover with hot syrup or other cooking liquid, leaving ¼″ head space. Apply lid and ring band. *To pack raw,* place fruit, cut side down in jar; cover with hot syrup or other liquid, leaving ¼″ head space. Apply lid and ring band.	15 min. 20 min. 20 min. 25 min.	
Persimmons		Freezing recommended; see chart on page 85.		
Plums and **fresh prunes** Duarte, Eldorado, Italian prune, Nubiana, President, Queen Anne, Santa Rosa, Stanley, Sugar, Wickson	1 to 1½ lbs.	Cut in half and remove pits, or leave whole and prick skins. Peel if desired (as for nectarines). *To pack hot,* drop fruit into syrup or other liquid; bring to a boil. Pack hot; cover with hot cooking liquid, leaving ¼″ head space. Apply lid and ring band. *To pack raw,* put fruit in jar; cover with hot syrup or other liquid, leaving ¼″ head space. Apply lid and ring band.	15 min. 15 min. 20 min. 20 min.	
Rhubarb	⅔ to 1 lb.	Cut ½″ lengths. Add ½ to 1 cup sugar to 1 quart fruit; mix and let stand 3 or 4 hours. Bring to a boil; pack hot, then cover with hot cooking liquid, leaving ¼″ head space. Apply lid and ring band.	10 min. 10 min.	
Tomatoes	1¼ to 2¼ lbs.	Dip in boiling water, then cold water; peel; cut out core. *To pack hot,* bring whole peeled tomatoes to a boil in very small amount of juice or water. Pack hot, then cover with hot cooking liquid, leaving ¼″ head space. Add 1 teaspoon lemon juice and ½ teaspoon salt to each pint. Apply lid and ring band. *To pack raw,* cut tomatoes in half. Pack, cut side down, filling jar to the top, pressing down after 4 halves are packed. Add hot cooking liquid, leaving ¼″ head space. Then add salt and lemon juice as above. Apply lid and ring band.	15 min. 15 min. 50 min. 50 min.	

JAMS, JELLIES & OTHER PRESERVES

Few treats are quite so tasty as homemade preserves spread on crisp toast or steaming hot biscuits—especially first thing in the morning. Most are easy to make; the simple key to success is to choose the freshest possible fruit.

Use your culinary imagination to "put up" sweets at home that are quite different from anything you can buy at the store. Their distinctive fruit flavors can enhance not only breakfast and lunch, but dinner, too, alongside meats and poultry.

"Preserves" have many tastes, many names

Fruits combined with sugar—usually boiled together—make the various types of preserves we enjoy. Don't let nomenclature confuse you; preserves fall under many names: jams, butters, marmalades, conserves, and one called just "preserves." They're all described below. Jelly—the clear, sparkling spread—is in a class by itself; directions for making jelly begin on page 27.

To get good flavor and consistency, you need the right proportions of fruit, sugar, pectin, and acid. Some fruits have enough pectin and acid to jell when cooked with sugar; others require the addition of pectin or an acid such as lemon juice, or both. And sometimes fruits low in either acid or pectin are combined with other fruits that supply them in the right proportions.

Jams are combinations of crushed or chopped fruit and sugar that are cooked to a fairly smooth consistency, thick enough to spread well. Berries and other soft fruits make good jams. Sometimes pectin and acid are added, depending on the fruit and the result desired.

With commercial pectin, a *short-boil method* is used and more sugar is required. Always follow the directions on the package of pectin you are using, since directions are not interchangeable from one brand to another. (For jams made without cooking, see page 89.)

Preserves are similar to jams, except that whole fruits or large pieces are used, and they are cooked in such a way that the fruit retains its shape. The surrounding syrup should be bright and clear and have a good spreading consistency.

Marmalades are soft jellies, usually containing thin, suspended pieces of citrus peel or fruit.

Conserves are like jam, except that usually two or more fruits are cooked together. Often they contain raisins and nuts.

Butters are simply fruit purées that are combined with sugar and cooked down slowly to a thick, spreading consistency. Less sugar is used in making them than in making most other preserves, and often spices are added for flavor.

What equipment is needed?

You'll need a cooking pot large enough to boil the fruit and sugar rapidly without their boiling over—one with a wide, flat bottom. A 6 to 8-quart pot is about right for most recipes.

Unless you plan to use up the preserves in a few weeks or to freeze them, they should be "put up" in regular canning jars (jars that can withstand the heat of boiling water) and covered with lids that can be sealed. Paraffin alone will not prevent spoilage in hot, dusty, humid areas. As with any canning, do not use jars that are chipped or cracked.

Step-by-step canning for jams, marmalades, preserves, conserves

1 Wash and sort fruit. Chop or slice it, or leave whole, according to recipe directions. Do not use overripe fruit.

2 Get out canning jars, lids, and ring bands. Check jar rims; discard any jars with nicks or cracks (see illustration on page 8). Discard rusted or bent ring bands. Sterilize jars by immersing them in water and boiling them for 15 minutes; keep them immersed in the hot water until ready to fill. Scald lids and ring bands. Keep lids in scalding hot water until used.

3 In the cooking pot, cook fruits in small batches as required in each recipe. **Do not try to double recipes; it doesn't work.**

4 Stirring frequently, bring fruit and its syrup to a quick boil. Watch that it doesn't boil over; this can happen quickly. Cook until thickened.

5 Pour into hot jars, skim off any foam, and add more fruit to within ⅛ to ¼ inch of top, depending on recipe. Wipe rims with a clean, damp cloth. Place lids on jars and screw on ring bands as tightly as you comfortably can. Let cool on a towel out of a draft; then press lids with your finger. If they stay down, they're sealed (see illustration on page 9). Label and store in a cool, dark area.

Jam & Other Preserve Recipes

Strawberry-Rhubarb Jam

In a happy marriage of flavors, rhubarb lends its special tang as strawberries contribute sweetness.

  1 **pound rhubarb**
  ¼ **cup water**
      About 4 cups fully ripe strawberries
  6½ **cups sugar**
  1 **pouch (3 oz.) liquid pectin**

Prepare 8 half-pint canning jars, following step 2 on page 12.

Rinse and thinly slice the unpeeled rhubarb and place in a pan; add water; bring to a boil. Reduce heat, cover pan, and simmer until rhubarb is soft (about 1 minute), stirring once or twice. Measure rhubarb. Thoroughly crush strawberries and add enough strawberries to rhubarb to make 3½ cups fruit. (Pack fruit solidly into cup to measure.) Turn the 3½ cups prepared rhubarb-strawberry mixture into a pot. Add sugar and stir until well blended.

Bring mixture to a full rolling boil. Stirring constantly, boil hard for 1 minute. Remove from heat and immediately stir in pectin. Skim off foam. Stir mixture for 5 minutes to cool slightly and to prevent fruit from floating, occasionally skimming off foam. Proceed according to step 5 (at left), filling to within ⅛ inch of rim. Makes 8 half pints.

Old-fashioned Strawberry Jam

As enticing to the eye as it is to the taste, this old-time classic has a clear, bright red color and a garden-fresh flavor.

  4 **cups crushed fresh strawberries**
  4 **cups sugar**

Prepare 4 half-pint canning jars, following step 2 on page 12.

Rinse and place strawberries in a 4 to 5-quart pot; stir in sugar until well blended. Bring mixture to a boil over high heat, stirring constantly. Continue boiling, uncovered and stirring frequently, for 10 to 15 minutes or until thickened. Proceed according to step 5 (at left), filling jars to within ⅛ inch of rim. Makes 4 half pints.

Easy Boysenberry Jam
(Pictured on pages 23 and 34)

Belying the notion that jam-making means long, hot hours in the kitchen, this perfectly simple delicacy cooks up in minutes. You can substitute fresh raspberries for boysenberries, if you like.

  3 **cups boysenberries or raspberries**
  3 **cups sugar**

Prepare 3 half-pint canning jars, following step 2 on page 12.

Rinse and crush berries and place in a 2-quart pan. Stir in sugar until well blended. Bring mixture to a boil over medium heat; continue to boil, uncovered and stirring occasionally, for 3 minutes or until thickened. Proceed according to step 5 (at left), filling jars to within ⅛ inch of rim. Makes 3 half pints.

MAKING JAM IN A MICROWAVE

Even if you've never had the slightest urge to put up jams, owning a microwave oven is reason enough to give it a try. So quick is the microwave method, you can even whip up a fresh batch of jam in the morning to serve warm for breakfast.

To avoid boil-over, use a generously oversized container for the syrup. Our favorite is a 2-quart (8-cup) glass measure. Since it requires no pot holders, it is easy to remove from the oven; its handle and spout simplify transferring the bubbly jam into hot, sterilized jars.

An alternative is to use a 2½ or 3-quart ceramic or glass casserole, but this will get hot, so keep thick pot holders handy.

Our basic microwave recipe, with its variations, makes 10 different fresh fruit jams. Refrigerated, these jams keep well for several months; freeze them for longer storage. If you prefer to can them, prepare two half-pint canning jars, following step 2 on page 12. Proceed according to step 5, filling to within ¼ inch of the rim.

Each batch of jam makes about 2 cups. As with conventionally made jam, recipe quantities should not be multiplied. If you have an abundance of fruit, consider making several batches. Or prepare measured amounts of fruit with sugar and flavorings, and freeze them. Later, thaw a portion and make fresh jam any time.

Basic Microwave Jam

Diced or crushed fruit and flavorings (recipes follow)
1½ cups sugar
½ teaspoon butter or margarine

Prepare fruit and flavorings and place in a 2-quart glass measure or 2½ to 3-quart casserole. Add sugar and butter. Let stand until juices form (about 30 minutes).

Microwave, uncovered, on HIGH (100% power) for 6 minutes or until mixture begins to boil. Stir through. Microwave on HIGH (100% power) for 10 to 13 minutes, stirring every 2 or 3 minutes. Spoon out 1 tablespoon into a custard cup, and refrigerate for 15 minutes; then test consistency. If you like your jam thicker, reheat jam to boiling, then microwave on HIGH (100% power) for 2 more minutes; retest consistency. Makes about 2 cups.

Apricot. Remove pits from about 1 pound **apricots**; chop to make 2 cups. Add 2 tablespoons **lemon juice**.

Apricot-pineapple. Remove pits from about ¾ pound apricots; chop to make 1½ cups. Combine with ½ cup canned **unsweetened crushed pineapple** or finely chopped fresh pineapple. Add 1 tablespoon **lemon juice.**

Berry. Crush about 3 cups **raspberries,** blackberries, boysenberries, or olallieberries; or use a combination of half raspberries and half of any of the black berries. You should have 2 cups. Add 1 tablespoon **lemon juice**.

Blueberry. Slightly crush about 3 cups **blueberries** to make 2 cups. Add ¼ cup **lemon juice**, ½ teaspoon grated **lemon peel**, and ¼ teaspoon **ground cinnamon**.

Strawberry. Crush about 3½ cups whole **strawberries** to make 2 cups. Add 1½ tablespoons **lemon juice**.

Cherry (sweet varieties). Pit about 1 pound **cherries** and cut into quarters to make 2 cups. Add ¼ cup **lemon juice**, ½ teaspoon grated **lemon peel**, and a 2-inch **cinnamon stick** (or ½ teaspoon ground cinnamon). Remove cinnamon stick after cooking.

Spiced fig-orange. Dice 8 to 10 **figs** to make 1½ cups; combine with ½ cup peeled, seeded, and chopped **orange** to make 2 cups. Add 1½ teaspoons grated **orange peel**, 3 tablespoons **lemon juice,** and ¼ teaspoon *each* ground **cloves** and **cinnamon**.

Peach or nectarine. Remove pits from about 1 pound **peaches** or nectarines; peel and chop to make 2 cups. Add 1 tablespoon **lemon juice**. If desired, stir in 2 drops **almond extract** after cooking.

Peach-plum marmalade. Remove pits from about ½ pound *each* **peaches** and **plums**; chop to make 1½ cups total. Combine with ½ cup finely chopped unpeeled **orange**.

Blueberry-Loganberry Jam

A sparkle of loganberry wine adds fantasy to the blueberry flavor of this richly hued jam.

1 **package (10 oz.) frozen unsweetened blueberries, thawed**
4 **cups sugar**
2 **cups loganberry wine**
2 **tablespoons frozen orange juice concentrate, thawed**
2 **pouches (3 oz. *each*) liquid pectin**

Prepare 7 half-pint canning jars, following step 2 on page 12.

Rinse and crush blueberries and place in a 2-quart pan. Stir in sugar, wine, and orange juice until well blended. Bring mixture to a boil over high heat, stirring constantly. Continue boiling, uncovered and stirring constantly, for 1 minute.

Remove from heat and stir in pectin all at once; skim off foam; let stand for about 6 minutes and then skim again. Proceed according to step 5 on page 13, filling jars to within ⅛ inch of rim. Makes 7 half pints.

Plum Jam

If you relish a touch of tart along with your sweet, plum jam may become your favorite spread.

About 2½ **pounds Santa Rosa or other firm ripe plums**
3½ **cups sugar**

Rinse plums and remove pits. Finely chop or force plums through a food chopper, to make 4 cups. Place plums in a 4-quart pot; stir in sugar until well blended. Let stand for 1 hour.

Prepare 4 half-pint canning jars, following step 2 on page 12.

Bring plum mixture to a boil over medium heat, stirring frequently. Continue cooking, uncovered and stirring occasionally, for about 20 minutes or until thickened. Proceed according to step 5 on page 13, filling jars to within ⅛ inch of rim. Makes 4 half pints.

Raspberry-Plum Jam

Here's a delicious and penny-wise way to extend raspberries when you want to make jam in quantity—combine them with more plentiful (and less expensive) plums.

About 2½ **pounds Santa Rosa or other firm ripe plums**
2 **packages (about 10 oz. *each*) frozen raspberries in syrup (thawed) or 3 cups fresh raspberries**
10 **cups sugar**
½ **cup lemon juice**
2 **pouches (3 oz. *each*) liquid pectin**

Prepare 12 half-pint canning jars, following step 2 on page 12.

Rinse plums and remove pits. Finely chop or force plums through a food chopper, to make 4 cups. Place plums and raspberries in an 8-quart pot. Stir in sugar and lemon juice until well blended.

Bring mixture to a boil over high heat, stirring constantly; boil, uncovered and stirring, for 1 minute. Remove from heat and immediately stir in pectin all at once; skim off foam. Proceed according to step 5 on page 13, filling jars to within ⅛ inch of rim. Makes 12 half pints.

Huckleberry Jam

The perfect celebration of a berrypicking bonanza, this jam can be reserved for unusual, attractive, and delectable Christmas gifts.

About 6 **cups huckleberries**
1 **package (2 oz.) powdered pectin**
8 **cups sugar**

Prepare 9 half-pint canning jars, following step 2 on page 12.

Rinse and crush berries. Measure 6 cups of the crushed fruit into a 6-quart pot. (If you do not have quite enough fruit, add water to fill last fraction of a cup.) Stir in pectin and bring to a boil over high heat, stirring constantly. Add sugar and continue stirring until mixture comes to a full rolling boil again. Let fruit boil for exactly 2 minutes. Remove from heat and skim off foam. Proceed according to step 5 on page 13, filling jars to within ⅛ inch of rim. Makes 9 half pints.

Note: To use a 1¾-ounce package of pectin instead of the 2-ounce size, make this change: after adding sugar, boil jam for just 1 minute, stirring constantly.

Cranberry-Orange Jam

This recipe offers you a choice of textures. It cooks down into a tangy, thick jam—or, for a smooth and glistening jelly, it can be poured through a jelly bag or small sterilized wire strainer when you fill the jars.

    1 pound cranberries
    3 cups water
    ¾ cup orange juice
    ¼ cup lemon juice
    4 cups sugar
    2 pouches (3 oz. *each*) liquid pectin

Prepare 6 half-pint canning jars, following step 2 on page 12.

Rinse cranberries well and place in a 5-quart pot. Add water and bring to a boil; reduce heat and simmer, uncovered, for 10 minutes. Drain well, reserving liquid. Place berries in a blender or food processor and whirl until puréed. Add enough reserved liquid to the berries to make 4 cups.

Return berries to kettle and stir in orange juice, lemon juice, and sugar until well blended. Bring mixture to a boil over high heat, stirring constantly; boil, uncovered, for 1 minute. Remove from heat and stir in pectin all at once. Skim off foam.

Proceed according to step 5 on page 13, filling jars to within ⅛ inch of rim. Makes 6 half pints.

Note: For best flavor, store for at least 1 week before using.

Pumpkin-Orange Jam

Pumpkin mellows the more acidic orange in this brilliantly colorful jam. Beautiful, unusual, and easy to prepare, it is a good candidate for gifts.

    2 medium-size oranges, rinsed
    2 cups sugar
    4 cups pumpkin, canned or freshly cooked

Grate outer layer of orange peels; set aside. Remove and discard inner white membrane of orange; finely chop pulp, to make about 1 cup. Place grated peel, pulp, and any juice in a 3-quart pan. Stir in sugar and pumpkin until well blended.

Bring mixture to a boil, reduce heat, and simmer, uncovered and stirring occasionally, for 30 minutes. Meanwhile, prepare 7 half-pint canning jars, following step 2 on page 12. Proceed according to step 5, filling jars to within ⅛ inch of rim. Makes 7 half pints.

Honeydew Jam

Mild honeydew pairs with wild ginger in this highly original combination of flavors. Try it as a relish alongside roasted pork or chicken.

    3 cups honeydew melon pieces (about 1-inch cubes)
    3 cups sugar
    3 tablespoons lemon juice
    1 tablespoon chopped candied ginger

Place melon pieces in a 3-quart pan. Stir in sugar, lemon juice, and candied ginger until well blended. Let stand for about 2 hours or until a syrup forms.

Bring mixture to a boil, stirring constantly, and continue to boil and stir for 2 minutes. Reduce heat and cook, uncovered and stirring frequently, for about 45 minutes or until mixture is thickened and melon is translucent.

Meanwhile, prepare 4 half-pint canning jars, following step 2 on page 12. Proceed according to step 5, filling jars to within ⅛ inch of rim. Makes 4 half pints.

Apple Butter

(Pictured on page 34)

Fragrant and spicy, apple butter is a semisoft spread whose full flavor is brought out by slow, even cooking. It's best to make apple butter in a heavy metal pot rather than a thin, light one, in order to maintain an even temperature. If Golden Delicious apples aren't available, use another variety; the apple butter will be sweeter or tarter, depending on the flavor of the fruit.

    3½ cups apple cider
    4 cups water
    8 large Golden Delicious apples, peeled, cored, and sliced
    1½ cups sugar
    ¼ teaspoon salt
    ¾ teaspoon ground cinnamon
    1 whole cinnamon stick

In a heavy 4 or 5-quart pot, combine cider and water. Bring to a boil over high heat. Add apples; reduce heat and simmer, uncovered and stirring occasionally, for 45 minutes.

Stir in sugar, salt, and ground and whole cinnamon until well blended. Cook over medium-low heat, uncovered and stirring occasionally, until mixture thickens to the consistency of hot applesauce (20 to 25 minutes). Remove and discard cinnamon stick.

Meanwhile, prepare 6 half-pint canning jars, following step 2 on page 12. Then proceed according to step 5, filling jars to within ¼ inch of rim. Makes 6 half pints.

Papaya Butter

You'll capture the essence of tropical papayas in this soft-spreading preserve. A hint of lime heightens its exotic flavor. Cook the fruit in a heavy metal pot, to maintain an even temperature.

 3 **large ripe papayas**
 ¼ **cup lime juice**
 1 **teaspoon grated lime peel**
 1½ **cups sugar**

Prepare 4 half-pint canning jars, following step 2 on page 12.

Remove peel and seeds from papayas; cut into small chunks. Whirl in a blender or food processor along with lime juice until smooth. Pour purée into a 4 or 5-quart pot and stir in lime peel and sugar until well blended. Bring to a boil; reduce heat and simmer, uncovered and stirring occasionally, until mixture thickens (about 5 minutes).

Proceed according to step 5 on page 13, filling jars to within ¼ inch of rim. Makes 4 half pints.

Caramel Spice Pear Butter

Spices and caramelized sugar enrich this soft spread with a distinctive and rather exotic flavor.

 About 15 Bartlett or other large, firm, ripe pears
 2 **cups water**
 6 **cups sugar**
 1 **teaspoon ground cloves**
 1½ **teaspoons ground cinnamon**
 ½ **teaspoon ground ginger**
 2 **tablespoons lemon juice**

Wash and core but do not peel pears. Slice and place in a 5-quart pot. Add water, cover, and cook over low heat for 30 minutes or until tender.

Let cool slightly and force through a food chopper or whirl in a food processor until finely chopped; return to kettle.

In a wide frying pan over medium heat, melt 1½ cups of the sugar, stirring often, until it caramelizes to a medium brown syrup. Pour immediately into pear pulp (syrup will sizzle and harden, but dissolve again as the preserves cook). Stir in remaining 4½ cups sugar, cloves, cinnamon, and ginger until well blended.

Bring mixture to a boil, reduce heat, and cook, uncovered, for about 45 minutes or until thickened. To prevent sticking, stir frequently as mixture begins to thicken. Stir in lemon juice just before removing from heat.

Meanwhile, prepare 9 half-pint canning jars, following step 2 on page 12. Proceed according to step 5, filling jars to within ⅛ inch of rim. Makes 9 half pints.

Apricot Butter

(Pictured on page 34)

If the apricot season showers you with abundance, you might quickly turn part of your bounty into purée.

 3 **pounds apricots**
 4 **tablespoons lemon juice**
 3 **cups sugar**

Prepare 5 half-pint canning jars, following step 2 on page 12.

Wash and pit apricots. Whirl apricots, a few at a time, in a blender or food processor until smooth, to make 4 cups. Pour purée into a 4-quart pot; stir in lemon juice and sugar until well blended. Bring mixture to a boil over high heat, stirring constantly. Continue boiling, uncovered and stirring frequently, for 15 to 18 minutes or until thickened.

Proceed according to step 5 on page 13, filling jars to within ⅛ inch of rim. Makes 5 half pints.

Apricot-Pineapple Butter

A deliciously tart flavor with just a hint of pineapple characterizes this fruit butter. Surprisingly, it uses apricot pits, too, in the first stage of cooking.

- 4 quarts rinsed, pitted, halved ripe apricots
- 12 apricot pits
- 1 cup water
- 5 cups sugar
- 2 cups sweetened or unsweetened crushed pineapple (do not drain)

Prepare 10 half-pint canning jars, following step 2 on page 12.

Place apricots, pits, and water in an 8-quart pot. Cook, uncovered and stirring occasionally, over low heat for about 1 hour and 15 minutes. Let cool slightly, remove and discard pits, and press fruit through a food mill or whirl in a food processor until finely chopped.

Return pulp to pan and cook, uncovered, over low heat for 10 to 15 minutes longer. Stir in sugar and pineapple until well blended. Bring mixture to a boil over high heat, stirring constantly. Proceed according to step 5 on page 13, filling jars to within ⅛ inch of rim. Makes 10 half pints.

Ginger Apple Preserves

For authoritative tartness, choose Pippins, Jonathans, or Winesaps for this hearty preserve. It makes as perfect a companion to meat as it does to a morning muffin.

- 5 cups sugar
- 2 cups water
- 8 or 9 large tart apples
- 2 tablespoons lemon juice
- 1 jar (about 5 oz.) candied ginger

Pour sugar into a heavy 5-quart pot; stir in water until well blended. Bring mixture to a boil over high heat, stirring often. Reduce heat to medium and cook, uncovered, for 10 to 15 minutes.

Pare and core apples; cut into ¼-inch-thick slices, to make about 8 cups. Sprinkle with lemon juice; mix well. Drain ginger, reserving syrup, and chop to make about ½ cup.

Add apples, ginger, and reserved syrup to sugar-water mixture. Cook (boiling gently) over medium heat, stirring occasionally, for 35 to 40 minutes or until preserve is thickened and apples are translucent.

Meanwhile, prepare 6 half-pint canning jars, following step 2 on page 12. Proceed according to step 5, filling jars to within ⅛ inch of rim. Makes 6 half pints.

Spiced Quince & Orange Preserves

Bubbling down to glorious, glistening goodness, quinces are enhanced in this preserve by orange slices, cinnamon, and cloves.

- 8 quinces
  About 5½ cups water
- 2 cups cider vinegar
- 6 cups sugar
- 3 medium-size unpeeled oranges, thinly sliced
- 3 sticks cinnamon, broken into 1-inch pieces
  About 30 whole cloves
- ⅛ teaspoon salt

Wash, peel, and remove cores from quinces. Place peels and cores in a 2-quart pan with 4 cups of the water.

Cut quinces into quarters; place in another pan containing about 1 inch of water (at least 1½ cups). Bring to a boil, cover, reduce heat, and simmer contents of both pans for about 30 minutes or until quinces are tender. Drain water from quinces; strain and reserve 1½ cups of the liquid from peels and cores and add to quinces. Discard peels, cores, and remaining liquid.

Stir in vinegar, sugar, orange slices (halved), cinnamon, cloves, and salt until well blended. Bring mixture to a boil over medium heat and continue to cook, stirring occasionally, until syrup is clear and slightly thickened; it will continue to thicken as it cools.

Meanwhile, prepare 8 half-pint canning jars, following step 2 on page 12. Proceed according to step 5, filling jars to within ⅛ inch of rim. Makes 8 half pints.

Proper canning equipment paves the way for canning success. Here are the basics (clockwise from top center): jelly bag, steam pressure canner, thermometer, colander, canning jars and lids, glass jelly thermometer, measuring cups, labels, wide-mouth funnel, jar lifter, and canning kettle with jar-filled rack. Details on these utensils appear on pages 5 and 6.

BRANDIED FRUIT

(Pictured on page 34)

Canning fruits in brandy syrup gives them much the same flavor as fruits brandied the old-fashioned way, in a stone crock. And canning is a much more reliable method.

Apricots, cherries, peaches, pears, plums, and seedless grapes are all well suited to canning with brandy. They make delicious desserts served plain or with ice cream, or spooned over a slice of pound cake. They're also excellent meat accompaniments.

Each of the following recipes makes 6 pints of fruit. Prepare the 6 pint-size canning jars and other canning equipment as directed in step 2 on page 8. The varieties of fruit recommended for canning in the chart on pages 10 and 11 are the best for canning with brandy, too.

Apricots

1¼ cups sugar
1 cup water
6 to 8 pounds firm ripe apricots
About 1¼ to 1½ cups brandy

To make the syrup, combine sugar and water in a pan, bring to a boil, and cook until sugar dissolves; keep hot.

To prepare apricots, wash, cut in half, discard pits, and treat fruit to prevent darkening (see "Protecting fruit colors," page 7). Drain fruit and pack firmly into hot jars, cavity sides down. Pour in about ¼ cup hot sugar syrup. Pour 3 to 4 tablespoons brandy over fruit (the amount depends on preference for a moderate or strong liqueur flavor). Add enough syrup to fill jars to within ½ inch of top. Proceed according to steps 6–13 on page 9, processing jars for 20 minutes. Makes 6 pints.

Sweet Cherries

Follow procedure for Brandied Apricots. Wash 6 to 8 pounds cherries and remove pits, if desired. Use brandy, or substitute kirsch. Process pint jars for 20 minutes.

Grapes

Follow procedure for Brandied Apricots. Wash 6 to 8 pounds Thompson seedless grapes and remove stems. Process pint jars for 15 minutes.

Peaches

Follow procedure for Brandied Apricots. Select 6 to 8 pounds peaches. Dip fruit into scalding water for ½ to 1 minute to loosen skin; immediately plunge into cold water. Peel, halve, and remove pits, and treat fruit to prevent darkening (see page 7). Process pint jars for 25 minutes.

Pears

Follow procedure for Brandied Apricots. Use 6 to 8 pounds pears. Peel, halve, cut out cores, and treat to prevent darkening (see page 7). Process pint jars for 25 minutes.

Plums

Follow procedure for Brandied Apricots. Wash 6 to 8 pounds plums; peel, then cut in half, and pit. Process pint jars for 20 minutes.

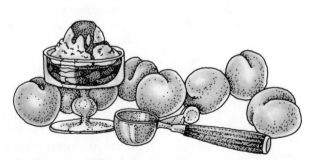

Apricot & Pear Conserve

Without disturbing a harmonious balance of flavors, pear, apricot, and lemon each asserts its individual character in this colorful conserve.

- 1 **cup (about 6 oz.) dried apricots, cut into thin slices**
- 1 **unpeeled lemon, thinly sliced and seeds removed (ends discarded)**
- 1 **cup water**
- 5 **cups rinsed, peeled, cored, and chopped firm ripe Anjou or Bosc pears (about 5 large)**
- 4 **cups sugar**

Place apricots in a small pan; stir in lemon slices and water. Bring mixture to a boil; reduce heat and simmer, uncovered, for 5 minutes; set aside.

Place pears in a 5-quart pot; stir in sugar until well blended. Bring mixture to a boil over medium heat, stirring occasionally. Continue cooking (boiling gently), uncovered and stirring occasionally, for 25 minutes. Stir in cooked apricot mixture (including liquid) and boil, uncovered and stirring occasionally, for 5 minutes longer or until reduced to about 5 cups.

Meanwhile, prepare 5 half-pint canning jars, following step 2 on page 12. Proceed according to step 5, filling jars to within ⅛ inch of rim. Makes 5 half pints.

Peach-Pineapple-Orange Conserve

Reminiscent of marmalade, this piquant medley of familiar fruits enhances ham and poultry at dinner or hot buttered toast at breakfast. You can use either syrup-packed pineapple or pineapple canned in its own juice—the latter will give a less sweet conserve.

- 8 to 10 **medium-size ripe peaches**
- 2 **medium-size oranges**
- 1 **can (about 8 oz.) crushed pineapple (do not drain)**
- 6 **cups sugar**

Rinse, peel, and pit peaches. Cut into pieces and whirl in a food processor or force through a food chopper just until chopped, to make 4 cups of fruit and juice.

Wash but don't peel oranges. Remove any seeds and finely chop. Place peach and orange pulps in a 6 or 7-quart pot; stir in crushed pineapple (including juice) and sugar until well blended. Cook over medium-low heat, uncovered

and stirring frequently, for about 35 minutes or until thickened.

Meanwhile, prepare 10 half-pint canning jars, following step 2 on page 12. Proceed according to step 5, filling jars to within ⅛ inch of rim. Makes 10 half pints.

Rhubarb Conserve

After letting rhubarb and sugar blend overnight, you finish the conserve with dates and raisins for extra fruity sweetness. Serve on toast, with meats, or over ice cream.

- 2½ **pounds rhubarb**
- 5½ **cups sugar**
- 2 **oranges**
- 1 **lemon**
- 1½ **cups *each* seedless raisins and chopped dates**
- 1 **cup chopped walnuts**

Wash rhubarb; cut off leaf and root ends, and dice to make 4 cups. Place rhubarb in a 5-quart pot; stir in sugar until well blended. Cover and let stand at room temperature overnight.

Cut unpeeled oranges and lemon into thin slices; remove seeds and then cut each slice into small pieces. Add orange and lemon pieces with dates and raisins to rhubarb-sugar mixture. Bring mixture to a boil; reduce heat and simmer, uncovered and stirring occasionally, for 35 to 40 minutes or until thickened. About 5 minutes before removing from heat, stir in walnuts.

Meanwhile, prepare 10 half-pint canning jars, following step 2 on page 12. Proceed according to step 5, filling jars to within ⅛ inch of rim. Makes 10 half pints.

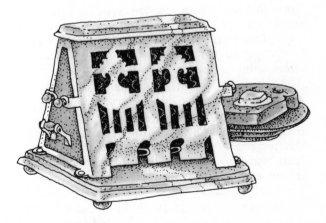

Fresh Fig Conserve

The crunch of walnuts combined with the zesty tang of orange peel makes this richly colored conserve a memorable taste experience.

2½ pounds fresh figs
2½ cups sugar
⅓ cup lemon juice
1 tablespoon grated orange peel
¼ cup chopped walnuts

Rinse figs; clip and discard fig stems; chop figs and place in a 5-quart pot. Stir in sugar until well blended and allow to stand for 1 hour.

Bring mixture to a boil over medium heat and cook, uncovered and stirring often, for about 20 minutes or until thickened. Stir in lemon juice, orange peel, and walnuts. Bring mixture to a boil again; boil, stirring often, for 3 minutes.

Meanwhile, prepare 5 half-pint canning jars, following step 2 on page 12. Proceed according to step 5, filling jars to within ⅛ inch of rim. Makes 5 half pints.

Pear-Pineapple Marmalade

While the flavor of pears reigns supreme in this marmalade, the three companion fruits contribute bright, sparkling color. When in season, firm ripe peaches can take the place of pears.

About 4 pounds firm ripe pears
1 large can (1 lb. 14 oz.) pineapple slices
2 large seedless oranges
About 12 cups sugar
1 small jar (4 oz.) maraschino cherries

Rinse and peel pears, remove cores, and slice thinly; cut each slice into about 4 pieces, to make 2 quarts. Drain pineapple and cut each slice into ¼-inch pieces. Cut unpeeled oranges into thin slices, then cut each slice into 4 wedges.

Combine fruits and add sugar; mix and let stand overnight at room temperature.

Pour mixture into a 4-quart pot and bring to a boil. Reduce heat and boil gently, uncovered and stirring occasionally, for about 1 hour or until fruit begins to look translucent. Drain cherries (reserve syrup for other uses) and finely chop; add to other fruits.

Meanwhile, prepare 10 half-pint canning jars, following step 2 on page 12. Proceed according to step 5, filling jars to within ⅛ inch of rim. Makes 10 half pints.

Quick Peach Marmalade

Plump fresh peaches join orange marmalade (either home-prepared or purchased) in this quick, sweet-tart preserve.

6 large peaches (about 3 lbs.)
¼ cup lemon juice
7½ cups sugar
½ teaspoon butter or margarine
1 pouch (3 oz.) liquid pectin
2 cups (1 pt.) orange marmalade

Prepare 10 half-pint canning jars, following step 2 on page 12.

Rinse and peel peaches; remove pits. Finely chop fruit or force through a food chopper (or whirl in a food processor). Place in a 4 or 5-quart pot; stir in lemon juice, sugar, and butter until well blended. Bring mixture to a boil over high heat, stirring constantly; boil for 1 minute. Remove from heat and immediately stir in all the pectin and orange marmalade. Let cool, stirring occasionally and skimming off any foam, for 5 minutes.

Proceed according to step 5 on page 13, filling jars to within ⅛ inch of rim. Makes 10 half pints.

Mandarin Marmalade

The distinctive, more-than-orange flavor of mandarin orange is emphasized in this marmalade. The bright, deep color adds to the attraction. Marmalade cooks best in a heavy metal pot.

5 or 6 Kinnow or Wilking mandarin oranges, rinsed
3 cups water
4½ cups sugar

Carefully peel oranges, keeping pieces of peel as large as possible; set peel aside.

Cut oranges in half crosswise; pick out and discard seeds. Whirl fruit in a blender or food processor to make 2 cups pulp. Place in a 4 or 5-quart pot and add water.

Cut enough of the reserved peel into julienne strips to make ½ cup. Add to pot along with sugar; stir until well blended. Bring to a boil over high heat, stirring constantly. Boil, uncov-

Plump purple boysenberries bubble down to syrupy goodness for topping toast, muffins, or pancakes. For jam recipe, see page 13.

ered and stirring occasionally, until mixture thickens and jell point is reached (about 40 minutes—see page 28). Remove from heat at once.

Meanwhile, prepare 4 half-pint canning jars, following step 2 on page 12. Proceed according to step 5, filling jars to within ¼ inch of rim. Makes 4 half pints.

Lemon Marmalade

For this exquisitely fresh and tart-tasting marmalade, you use only the thin yellow surface peel of the lemons.

About 11 medium-size lemons, rinsed
½ **cup water**
6 **cups sugar**
1 **pouch (3 oz.) liquid pectin**

Use a sharp knife to slice off all the thin outer yellow peel from lemons; cut peel into slivers. Then ream juice from lemons. You should have 1¾ cups peel and 2 cups lemon juice.

Place peel, water, and ½ cup of the lemon juice in a 3-quart pan. Bring to a boil; reduce heat, cover, and simmer, stirring occasionally, for about 25 minutes or until peel is tender and translucent.

Stir in remaining lemon juice and sugar until well blended. Bring to a full rolling boil over high heat, stirring constantly. Remove from heat, cover, and let stand at room temperature for 18 to 24 hours.

Prepare 4 half-pint canning jars, following step 2 on page 12.

Rapidly return marmalade to boiling, stirring to prevent sticking. Stir in pectin all at once and boil, stirring constantly, for exactly 1 minute. Remove from heat and quickly skim off any foam. Proceed according to step 5 on page 13, filling jars to within ⅛ inch of rim. Makes 4 half pints.

Bittersweet Marmalade

If you like wide-awake flavors at breakfast, try this particularly tart marmalade, brewed from whole peels of oranges, lemons, and grapefruit.

6 **medium-size thin-skinned oranges**
2 *each* **lemons and medium-size grapefruit, both with thin skins**
2 **cups water**
9 **cups sugar**

Cut unpeeled, rinsed oranges, lemons, and grapefuit into ⅛-inch slices, discarding seeds and end pieces. Cut orange and lemon slices in quarters and cut grapefruit slices in eighths.

Place oranges, lemons, grapefruit, and water in a 6 or 7-quart pot. Bring mixture to a boil; reduce heat, cover, and simmer for 25 to 30 minutes or until peel is tender and translucent. Stir in sugar until well blended. Cook over medium-high heat, uncovered and stirring often, for about 30 minutes until mixture thickens and reaches jell point (see "Finding the magic jell point" on page 28). Remove from heat, cover, and let stand at room temperature for 18 to 24 hours.

Prepare 16 half-pint canning jars, following step 2 on page 12.

Rapidly return marmalade to a boil, stirring to prevent sticking. Proceed with step 5 on page 13, filling jars to within ⅛ inch of rim. Makes 16 half pints.

Pumpkin-Orange Marmalade

Golden and translucent, bits of pumpkin mingle with orange and lemon in a marmalade that's lighter and fresher than most all-citrus versions.

1 *each* **medium-size orange and lemon**
3 **cups water**
1 **small pumpkin (about 3 lbs.)**
4 **cups sugar**

Thinly slice unpeeled orange and lemon, remove seeds and discard end pieces; cut slices into quarters. Place in a 4 or 5-quart pot and add water. Bring mixture to a boil; reduce heat, cover, and simmer for about 25 minutes or until orange peel is tender.

Meanwhile, peel pumpkin and cut away blossom and stem ends. Cut into strips about ½ inch wide and ⅛ inch thick; then cut strips into ½-inch squares, to make about 2 quarts.

Stir sugar into citrus mixture until well blended; add pumpkin pieces. Bring mixture to boiling over high heat, stirring constantly. Reduce heat to medium and continue cooking, uncovered and stirring frequently, for about 40 minutes until mixture thickens and reaches the jell point (see "Finding the magic jell point" on page 28). Cover and let stand at room temperature for 18 to 24 hours.

Prepare 4 half-pint canning jars, following step 2 on page 12.

Return marmalade to a full, rolling boil over medium heat, stirring often to prevent sticking; boil for 1 minute.

Proceed according to step 5 on page 13, filling jars to within ⅛ inch of rim. Makes 4 half pints.

Pineapple-Orange Marmalade

A tropical-tasting blend of pineapple, orange, and fresh ginger results in this zesty and exotic rendition of marmalade.

1 large pineapple (about 5 lbs.)
1 large orange
2 tablespoons minced fresh ginger
3 cups sugar

Remove rind and core from pineapple; finely chop fruit to make about 4½ cups. Rinse and finely chop unpeeled orange, removing seeds. Place pineapple and orange in a 5-quart pot. Stir in ginger and sugar until well blended.

Bring mixture to boiling; reduce heat and cook, uncovered and stirring often, for about 25 minutes or until thickened.

Meanwhile, prepare 6 half-pint canning jars, following step 2 on page 12. Proceed according to step 5, filling jars to within ⅛ inch of rim. Makes 6 half pints.

Spicy Tomato Marmalade

(Pictured on page 34)

It may surprise you that the humble tomato wends its juicy way not only into the catsup jar but into the jam jar as well. Rich with bright citrus flavor and enlivened by spices, tomatoes actually do cook into delicious marmalade.

4 to 5 pounds fully ripe tomatoes
1 *each* orange and lemon
¼ cup cider vinegar
1½ teaspoons *each* ground cinnamon and allspice
¾ teaspoon ground cloves
3 cups sugar

Rinse, peel, core, and coarsely chop tomatoes, to make 8 cups. With a vegetable peeler, carefully remove thin outer peel from orange and lemon; cut peel into julienne strips. Holding fruit over a bowl to catch juice, cut and discard remaining peel and white membrane from orange and lemon; coarsely chop fruit.

Place tomatoes, orange, lemon (plus any juice), and peel in a 5-quart pot. Stir in vinegar, cinnamon, allspice, cloves, and sugar until well blended. Bring mixture to a boil; reduce heat and simmer, uncovered, for about 2 hours or until reduced to about 2 pints. Stir occasionally to prevent sticking.

Prepare 4 half-pint canning jars, following step 2 on page 12. Proceed according to step 5, filling jars to within ⅛ inch of rim. Makes 4 half pints.

Marmalade in Candied Shells

(Pictured on page 26)

Here's a novel and cheerful way to show off freshly prepared citrus marmalade: place it in a candied orange shell. These sugar-frosted shells will stay fresh for several weeks in the refrigerator and, when empty of marmalade, can be sliced and eaten.

5 medium-size oranges, unpeeled
2 small lemons
3 cups water
6 cups sugar
½ cup lemon juice
4 candied shells (recipe follows), optional

Rinse and thinly slice oranges and lemons, discarding seeds. Place in a 5-quart pot, cover with water, and let stand overnight.

Bring to a boil and cook, uncovered, for 40 minutes. Remove from heat and let stand for 4 hours. Stir in sugar until well blended; bring to a boil over high heat, stirring constantly. Continue boiling, stirring occasionally, until mixture thickens and reaches the jell point (about 20 minutes—see page 28). Remove from heat and stir in the lemon juice.

Meanwhile, prepare 7 half-pint canning jars, following step 2 on page 12. Then proceed according to step 5, filling jars to within ⅛ inch of rim. Or, serve in candied shells as directed below. Makes 7 half pints.

Candied orange shells. Wash 4 large oranges and cut a ½-inch-thick lid off the top of each. With a curved grapefruit knife, cut fruit pulp away from rind, scraping any remaining mem-

brane from rind with a heavy spoon. Scrape fruit pulp off lid. (Reserve fruit pulp for other uses.) Cover shells and lids with cold water; bring to a boil and cook for 20 minutes. Drain well; cool shells.

In a 4-quart pot, combine 6 cups *each* **sugar** and **water.** Add 6 tablespoons **glycerine** (available at drug stores); heat until sugar dissolves. Add shells and lids; bring to a boil over medium-high heat and boil, uncovered, until syrup is medium thick (220°F on a candy thermometer). Let shells and lids stand in syrup 24 hours, turning them several times.

Bring syrup to a boil again and boil over medium-high heat until syrup is thick (232°F), turning shells over several times to prevent scorching. Remove shells and lids from syrup carefully; turn each upside down over an inverted paper cup to drain and cool. When cool enough to handle, roll in granulated sugar, coating completely. Cool thoroughly, fill with marmalade, and secure lids with wooden picks.

How to make jelly

Beautifully bright and transparent, jelly should be tender enough to spread even as it holds its jiggly shape.

Jellies are fruit juices cooked with sugar until the "jell point" is reached (see page 28). You start by extracting the juice and then straining it to make clear and sparkling jelly. For jellies of the right consistency, you'll need to use just the right proportions of sugar, fruit, pectin, and acid.

Sound, ripe fruit is the essence of good jelly. Underripe fruit contains more pectin than ripe fruit does, but ripe fruit is needed for full sweetness and flavor. The dilemma is not serious—you just add pectin to the fruits that need it.

The juice from these fruits usually contains enough pectin and acid for jelly:

Apples, tart

Blackberries, tart

Crabapples

Cranberries

Currants

Gooseberries

Lemons

Loganberries

Plums, most varieties

Prunes, sour

Quinces

The juice from these fruits usually is low in acid or pectin:

Apples, sweet

Blackberries, sweet

Cherries, Sour

Elderberries

Grapefruit

Grape juice, eastern Concord

Grapes, California

Loquats

Oranges

The juice from these fruits always needs added acid or pectin, or both:

Apricots

Figs

Grapes, western Concord

Guavas

Peaches

Pears

Pomegranates

Prunes

Raspberries

Strawberries

If you need extra pectin

Pectin is what causes jelling. Underripe fruit contains more pectin than fully ripe fruit but lacks full flavor. Overripe fruit doesn't contain enough pectin; its use results in runny jelly.

Here's a way to test the pectin content of fruit juice. Add 1 teaspoon of cooked fruit juice to 1 tablespoon rubbing alcohol (70 percent alcohol). Stir to mix—*do not taste!* Juices rich in pectin will form a jellylike mass that can be picked up with a fork. Juices low in pectin will form only a few pieces of jellylike material. If more pectin is needed, you either add a commercial pectin or mix the juice with another fruit juice of higher pectin content. Discard the alcohol test.

If pectin is to be added, add 1 tablespoon liquid pectin to 1 cup fruit juice. Test again for jelling. If more pectin is needed, add another tablespoonful and test again. Repeat until the test indicates that enough pectin has been added. Measure the remaining juice and add pectin.

Testing for enough acid

A tart juice is necessary for a good-tasting jelly. Compare the tartness of the juice with a mixture of 1 teaspoon lemon juice added to 3 tablespoons water and ½ teaspoon sugar. If the juice is not as tart as the lemon mixture, add 1 tablespoon lemon juice to each cup of fruit juice.

Sweeteners

Besides contributing to the flavor of fruit spreads, sugar—either beet or cane—aids in gel

Dainty candied orange shell makes an edible jam jar for marmalade of the same fruit—the perfect condiment for a light breakfast of croissants and soft-cooked eggs. The recipe is on page 25.

formation and also acts as a preservative. Sugar substitutes such as light corn syrup and honey may also be used in making jams and jellies.

Finding the magic jell point

The easiest way to tell when jelly has reached the jell point is to use a jelly thermometer (a glass tube calibrated to measure the jelling power of fruit juice) or an accurate thermometer. When its temperature reaches 228°F, the jelly is ready. (This is at sea level. To test at your elevation, boil water to see at what temperature it boils; then add 8°F for the jell point.)

Boil rapidly until jell point is reached

If you have no thermometer, dip a cool metal spoon into the boiling juice. Life it out and watch how the juice runs off the side of the spoon.

When the juice has almost reached the jell point, it will slowly come together and fall off the spoon in two drops. When it slides off the spoon in a sheet, the jelly is ready; remove from heat immediately (see illustration above).

Or you can put a little jelly on a plate in the refrigerator. If it jells in a few minutes, the jelly is ready. Be sure to take the jelly off the heat while you make the test.

Step-by-step canning for jelly

1 Get out canning jars, lids, and ring bands. Check jar rims; discard any jars with nicks or cracks (see illustration on page 8). Discard any rusted or bent ring bands. Immerse canning jars or jelly glasses in water and boil for 15 minutes to sterilize. Keep jars in the hot water until ready to use. Scald lids and ring bands; keep lids in scalding hot water until used.

2 Wash ripe fruit, removing stems and spoiled parts. Do not core or peel apples or other firm fruits—cut them into small pieces or force through a food choper. If fruit is soft, crush it to start the juice flowing.

3 To extract the juice, put crushed or cut fruit into a pan. To firm fruit—such as apples— you will need to add about 1 cup water for each pound of fruit; to each pound of semifirm fruit—such as plums—add about ¼ cup water. Soft fruits usually don't need water, but overripe fruit often needs about ¼ cup water for each pound of fruit. Whatever the fruit, add only enough water to prevent scorching, since the juice shouldn't be diluted any more than necessary.

Bring fruit to a boil; reduce heat to medium and cook for 5 to 10 minutes or until tender. Too much boiling reduces the jelling strength.

4 Pour fruit mixture through four thicknesses of wet, washed cheesecloth spread over a colander, or pour into a regular jelly bag made of strong muslin. Twist bag or cheesecloth and

Pour through cheesecloth-lined colander or through jelly bag

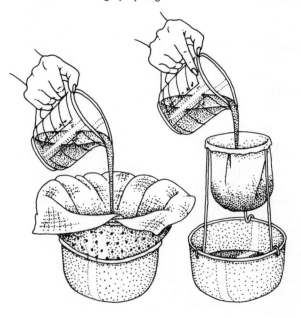

press out juice. To make very clear jelly, let juice drip into a pan without squeezing bag or cloth.

5 You can use one of two methods to make jelly.

The long-boil method uses a little less sugar. Follow recipe. Or if not using a recipe, you'll need to test the cooked juice for amount of natural fruit pectin and acid, supplying more of either or both if needed. (See page 27 for how to test and adjust juice's pectin and acid content.)

Cook only 4 to 6 cups juice at a time, using a kettle that holds 4 to 5 times the amount of juice to be cooked (1 cup juice plus 1 cup sugar makes 1¼ cups jelly). A small piece of butter added to the juice tends to keep it from boiling over and reduces foam.

When fruit juice comes to a boil, add the sugar and stir until dissolved. The amount of sugar you use will depend on the pectin and acid content of the juice. A good general rule is to use about ¾ to 1 cup sugar for juice with a high proportion of pectin (or ⅔ to ¾ cup for juice containing only a moderate amount of pectin) to each cup of fruit juice (see chart on pages 10 and 11).

Boil juice rapidly until the jell point is reached. Flavor, color and jelling ability are lost if jelly is allowed to boil too long.

The short-boil method depends on the use of commercial pectin and requires a higher proportion of sugar. The boiling time, usually about 1 minute, cannot be varied from the recipe or package directions. Follow the directions, then proceed to step 6 below.

6 If you use the short-boil method, remove jelly from heat immediately when time is up. If you use the long-boil method, remove it when the jell point is reached. Let stand a minute to allow foam to form; then carefully skim off the foam. Pour hot jelly quickly into hot jars, filling jars to within about ⅛ inch of tops. Carefully wipe off rim of jar. Put lid on each jar as it is filled, screwing ring band on as tightly as you comfortably can.

Cool jars away from drafts on a towel. Then press lids with your finger. If they stay down, they're sealed (see illustration on page 9). Label and store in a cool, dark area.

Jelly Recipes

Lime Mint Jelly
(Pictured on page 34)

Fresh lime juice and finely chopped mint leaves make an outstanding flavor combination. Since neither ingredient is too sweet, this jelly makes a good accompaniment for any meat—especially spring lamb.

    8 to 10 limes, rinsed
    4 cups sugar
    1¾ cups water
       Green food coloring (optional)
    1 pouch (3 oz.) liquid pectin
    3 tablespoons finely chopped mint
       leaves

Prepare 5 half-pint canning jars, following step 1 on page 28.

Grate zest (colored part of peel) from 5 limes; set aside. Squeeze out lime juice, using remaining limes as needed, to make ¾ cup juice. Pour juice, sugar, and water into a 4 or 5-quart pot and stir until blended. Bring mixture to a boil over medium-high heat, stirring occasionally. (At this point, stir in enough food coloring, if used, to get the desired tint.)

Pour in pectin all at once, stirring constantly. Add grated lime zest and the mint leaves. Boil vigorously, uncovered and stirring constantly, for 30 seconds.

Proceed with step 6 (at left), filling jars to within ¼ inch of rim. Makes 5 half pints.

Note: To use the 1¾-ounce package of powdered pectin, follow recipe above but boil for 1 minute after adding sugar, and do not boil after adding lime zest and mint.

Loquat Jelly

Though not a well-known fruit, loquats are ideal for jelly-making. The small, loosely clustered yellow fruits appear on large shrubs or trees in the spring; they are sweet, aromatic, and slightly acidic—similar in flavor to cooked plums.

    8 to 10 pounds loquats, rinsed
    2 cups water
    1½ cups lemon juice
    1 package (2 oz.) powdered pectin
    5 cups sugar

Place loquats in a 6 or 7-quart pot along with water and 1 cup of the lemon juice. Bring to a boil over high heat, stirring occasionally. Reduce heat to medium and cook, uncovered and stirring occasionally, until loquats are cooked to a saucelike consistency (about 40 minutes).

Pour through a strainer lined with a single layer of cheesecloth, pressing down on pulp and pits to yield the maximum amount of juice (you will need 4 cups of juice; the loquats may yield more, depending on the size of the fruit). Discard pulp and pits.

Prepare 7 half-pint canning jars, following step 1 on page 28.

Place 4 cups of the loquat juice in a 3 or 4-quart pot along with remaining ½ cup lemon juice and pectin. Bring to a boil over high heat, stirring often. Add sugar all at once, stirring constantly, and bring to a full boil again. Boil, uncovered and stirring constantly, for 2 minutes.

Proceed with step 6 on page 29, filling jars to within ⅛ inch of rim. Makes 7 half pints.

Note: To use the 1¾-ounce package of powdered pectin, follow recipe above but boil for 1 minute after adding the sugar.

Herb-Apple Jelly

Apple jelly with an unusual hint of a favorite herb is a thoughtful holiday gift. Made with bottled apple juice and dry herbs, this jelly takes so little time that it makes a good last-minute or any-season project. Take your pick of four different herbs—thyme, basil, rosemary, or mint. If you prefer a stronger flavor after tasting the herb mixture, let it stand longer than the prescribed time.

> 2 cups filtered apple juice
> ¼ cup dry thyme leaves (or substitute ⅓ cup dry basil, 2 tablespoons dry rosemary, or ¼ cup dry mint leaves)
> 3 tablespoons lemon juice
> ¼ teaspoon butter or margarine
> 3½ cups sugar
>   Red or green food coloring (optional)
> 1 pouch (3 oz.) liquid pectin

In a 4 or 5-quart pot, heat apple juice to a boil; remove from heat. Stir in thyme; cover and let stand for 30 minutes (for basil, 2 hours; for rosemary, 15 minutes; for mint, 10 minutes.)

Meanwhile, prepare 4 half-pint canning jars, following step 1 on page 28.

Pour mixture through a jelly bag or a cheesecloth-lined strainer; squeeze out and reserve all the liquid; discard herbs. Rinse pot and return liquid to pot. Stir in lemon juice, butter,

sugar, and a few drops of food coloring, if used. Bring to a boil over high heat, stirring constantly. Add pectin all at once and return to a full rolling boil. Boil for 1 minute, stirring constantly.

Proceed according to step 6 on page 29, filling jars to within ⅛ inch of rim. Makes 4 half pints.

Spicy Pepper Jelly

(Pictured on facing page)

Bright red or green bell peppers give a delightfully assertive flavor to this jelly. Serve either as a festive accompaniment to meat or as a topping for crackers spread with cream cheese.

> 4 large green or red bell peppers, seeded and cut into pieces
> 2½ cups vinegar
> 6 cups sugar
> 2 pouches (3 oz. *each*) liquid pectin

Prepare 6 half-pint canning jars, following step 1 on page 28.

Place pieces of pepper in a blender or food processor and whirl until finely chopped. Pour into a 5-quart pot and stir in vinegar and sugar until well blended. Bring to a rolling boil over high heat, stirring constantly. Pour in pectin, all at once, and return to a boil; cook, uncovered and stirring frequently, until thickened (about 3 minutes). Remove from heat and skim off foam.

Proceed according to step 6 on page 29, filling jars to within ⅛ inch of rim. Makes 6 half pints.

Jalapeño Pepper Jelly

Similar to spicy pepper jelly (preceding), this hotter version can be made to suit your taste— just remove some or all of the fiery hot seeds in the jalapeño peppers. Our testers generally preferred about half of the seeds removed.

>   About 5 medium-size whole canned jalapeño chile peppers
> ½ cup seeded, chopped green pepper
> ¼ cup seeded, chopped red bell pepper (or additional green pepper)
> 6 cups sugar
> ½ cups cider vinegar
> 2 pouches (3 oz. *each*) liquid pectin

(Continued on page 32)

Piquant pepper jellies, sparkling like jewels in the firelight, perk up a wintry evening. Cool cream cheese complements their zesty flavors. The recipe appears on this page.

Prepare 7 half-pint canning jars, following step 1 on page 28.

Rinse jalapeño peppers, discarding stem ends, any bits of blackened skin, and about half of the seeds. Chop peppers to make about ¼ cup. Place in a blender or food processor along with green and red pepper; whirl until finely chopped.

Pour into a 5-quart pot and stir in sugar and vinegar until well blended. Bring to a rolling boil over high heat, stirring constantly. Stir in pectin, all at once; return to boiling and boil, uncovered and stirring constantly, for 1 minute. Remove from heat; skim off foam.

Proceed according to step 6 on page 29, filling jars to within ⅛ inch of rim. Makes 7 half pints.

Quince Jelly

Resembling apples except for a misshapen stem end, quinces are grown primarily for jellymaking and preserving. Because of its high pectin content, juice from quinces jells easily and has a delicately light flavor.

8 cups peeled, cored, and coarsely chopped quinces
6 cups water
3 cups sugar

Place quinces in a 5-quart pot, add water, and bring to a boil over medium-high heat. Reduce heat and simmer gently, uncovered and stirring

USING PARAFFIN TO SEAL JELLY

By far the most reliable method of sealing preserves is to put them in regular canning jars with lids that seal (see page 5). However, paraffin can be used if jams and jellies are stored in a cool, dry place and used within a few months. (Changes in temperature may cause jelly to seep up around paraffin.)

To use paraffin, pour hot jelly into hot jelly glasses to within ½ inch of the top instead of ⅛ inch as called for in regular canning jars that seal. Cover quickly with a thin layer of hot paraffin (about ⅛ inch thick); immediately tip each glass slightly and rotate it to make a good seal around the edge. Let glasses stand until the thin layer of wax hardens; prick any bubbles that form on the surface. Place tops on the jars.

occasionally, until soft (about 45 minutes). Pour through a jelly bag or cheesecloth-lined strainer and let juice drain gradually into a bowl. Do not squeeze bag or jelly may be cloudy.

Prepare 4 half-pint canning jars, following step 1 on page 28.

Measure 4 cups of juice and return to pot (discard pulp). Stir in sugar until well blended. Boil rapidly over high heat, stirring often, until mixture thickens and reaches jell point (see page 28). Remove from heat immediately.

Proceed according to step 5, using the long-boil method; then continue with step 6, filling jars to within ⅛ inch of rim. Makes 4 half pints.

Pomegranate Jelly

The sweet-tart flavor of this bright red jelly comes from pomegranates. Allow a little extra time for preparation—you'll need to make almost a quart of fresh juice from the pomegranate seeds.

3½ cups pomegranate juice, fresh, frozen and thawed (directions follow), or bottled
¼ cup lemon juice
1 package (2 oz.) powdered pectin
4½ cups sugar

Prepare 6 half-pint canning jars, following step 1 on page 28.

Combine pomegranate juice, lemon juice, and pectin in a 4 or 5-quart pot. Bring to a boil over medium-high heat, stirring constantly. Stir in sugar until well blended; return to a boil and continue boiling, uncovered and stirring occasionally, for 2 minutes.

Proceed according to step 6 on page 29, filling jars to within ⅛ inch of rim. Makes 6 half pints.

Pomegranate juice. Cut the crown off each pomegranate and lightly score the peel lengthwise down the sides in several places. Submerge the scored fruit in a bowl or sink full of cold water and let soak at least 5 minutes. Holding the fruit under water, break sections apart with your fingers and separate the seeds from the pulp; as you work, the seeds will sink to the bottom and the peel and pulp will float. With a wire strainer, skim off and discard the peel and pulp.

Whirl about 1½ cups pomegranate seeds at a time in a blender or food processor until liquified. Pour through a jelly bag or cheesecloth-lined strainer and let juice drain gradually. (Or, to speed the straining, press juice through the cheesecloth; wear rubber gloves to avoid staining hands.) Store in refrigerator up to 5 days, or

SUNSHINE PRESERVES

Some of our grandparents used to make preserves by harnessing the radiant energy of the summer sun. The method is just as effective today. Apricot halves, nectarine and peach slices, and whole berries—such as blackberries, blueberries, currants, and raspberries—retain their plump shapes when cooked in this gentle manner.

You begin the process on the range, heating fruit and sugar together. Then you pour the mixture into wide, shallow pans or trays, which you arrange in full sun on a table or rack.

Preserves need frequent stirring while they thicken. Thickening time depends on the heat of your sun. In two of *Sunset's* tests, it took 10 hours in Seattle and just 2 hours in Phoenix.

Sunshine Preserves retain remarkably fresh fruit flavor and are less sweet than more conventional preserves. Though they're at their very best when eaten still warm from the sun, they can also be stored for later use.

Sunshine Apricot Preserves

About 2 pounds firm ripe apricots
3 cups sugar
2 tablespoons lemon juice

Wash apricots and cut into halves or quarters; discard pits. Measure 4 cups of the fruit and combine with the sugar and lemon juice in a 4 or 5-quart pot; stir gently to mix. Cover and let stand at room temperature for 1 hour. Over medium heat, bring mixture to a boil, stirring constantly. Turn heat to high and boil vigorously, uncovered, for 4 minutes without stirring. Remove from heat and let cool, uncovered, for 30 minutes.

Pour mixture into shallow glass or metal baking pans, foil roasting pans, or rigid plastic trays so that syrup around fruit is at least ⅓ inch deep but no deeper than ¾ inch. Cover with clear plastic wrap or a sheet of glass, leaving a 1-inch-wide opening along one side. Place pan in direct sunlight. Gently stir mixture and turn fruit pieces over every hour.

Remove preserves from sun when fruit is plump and syrup is thickened to about the consistency of corn syrup; preserves will thicken slightly more as they cool. It will take 2 to 10 hours, or more, depending on the heat of the sun. You may need to bring preserves in at night and then return them to the sun the following day. Serve at once or store according to directions that follow. Makes 3 cups.

Peach or nectarine preserves. Cut peeled peaches or peeled or unpeeled nectarines into ½-inch-thick slices; discard pits. Follow recipe for Sunshine Apricot Preserves, but increase lemon juice to ¼ cup.

Apple preserves. Cut peeled, cored apples into ½-inch-thick rings. Follow recipe for Sunshine Apricot Preserves, adding ½ teaspoon ground cinnamon.

Berry preserves. For whole blackberries, blueberries, boysenberries, gooseberries, raspberries, and strawberries (stems removed), follow recipe for Sunshine Apricot Preserves.

Currant preserves. Remove and discard stems. Follow recipe for Sunshine Apricot Preserves, but decrease sugar to 2½ cups.

Storing sunshine preserves

Spoon preserves into jars and cover; when refrigerated they will keep for at least 4 weeks. Or pack into freezer containers to within 1 inch of top, seal, and freeze.

Prepare 3 half-pint canning jars, following step 2 on page 8. Then proceed with steps 3 and 5–13, page 8, processing for 10 minutes. Makes 3 half pints.

. . . Pomegranate Jelly (cont'd.)

freeze. You'll get about 3½ cups juice from 7 or 8 medium-size pomegranates.

Huckleberry Jelly

Huckleberries resemble blueberries except that their seeds are larger; they are often more expensive, too. Either type of berry works well in this jelly, though most cooks prefer to save blueberries for eating or special baking and to use huckleberries for jelly-making.

> 8 **cups huckleberries (or blueberries)**
> 1 **cup water**
> 2 **tablespoons** *each* **orange juice and lemon juice**
> 1 **package (2 oz.) powdered pectin**
> 4½ **cups sugar**

Prepare 6 half-pint canning jars, following step 1 on page 28.

Here's holiday bounty from the kitchen... **1.** miniature pickled onions (page 54); **2.** strawberry sauce (page 84); **3.** brandied cherries (page 20); **4.** lemon-mint vinegar (page 59); **5.** mincemeat (page 67); **6.** tarragon & garlic vinegar (page 59); **7.** basil-oregano vinegar (page 59); **8.** a festive quartet including apple butter (page 16), apricot butter (page 17), tomato marmalade (page 25), and lime mint jelly (page 29); **9.** grape & rosemary vinegar (page 59); **10.** brandied peaches (page 20); **11.** basket brimming with easy raspberry jam (page 13) and papaya-plum chutney (page 61).

In a 4 or 5-quart pot, combine berries, water, orange juice, and lemon juice. Bring to a boil over high heat, stirring constantly. Reduce heat and simmer, uncovered, for 3 minutes; cool slightly.

Pour through a jelly bag or cheesecloth-lined strainer and let juice drain. Squeeze bag gently to release all the juice. Measure 3½ cups juice into a large pot. (If you don't have enough juice, add water to make up the difference.) Stir in pectin until well blended. Bring to a boil over high heat, stirring constantly.

Stir in sugar and return mixture to a rolling boil. Boil for exactly 2 minutes. Remove from heat and skim off foam. Proceed with step 6 on page 29, filling jars to within ⅛ inch of rim. Makes 6 half pints.

Note: To use the 1¾-ounce package of powdered pectin, follow the recipe above but boil jelly for 1 minute after adding sugar, stirring constantly.

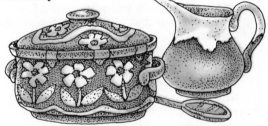

Wine Jelly

The mellow wine flavors of these jellies complement both meats and cheeses. You might offer it as a condiment with poultry, especially. Or at hors d'oeuvre time, pass wine jelly along with cream cheese to spread on crackers.

The best wines for making jelly are those with a full natural flavor and body, though any wine may be used. Here are some suggestions: for a deep red jelly, try a mellow Port, such as Ruby Port, or a robust red table wine, such as Pinot Noir or Zinfandel. For a soft rosy jelly, pick a fruity Rosé wine, such as Grenache Rosé.

> 1¾ **cups (4/5 pt.) wine**
> 3 **cups sugar**
> 1 **pouch (3 oz.) liquid pectin**

Prepare 4 half-pint canning jars or jelly glasses, following step 1 on page 28.

Mix wine and sugar in top of a double boiler. Place over boiling water; stir until sugar is completely dissolved (about 5 minutes). Remove from heat, but leave jelly over hot water. Stir in pectin all at once. If foam forms on top, skim it off with a metal spoon. Proceed according to step 6 on page 29. Makes 4 half pints.

CANNING VEGETABLES

When your garden overflows with summer's bounty and there's more produce than you and your family can possibly eat, you have three choices: give it away to friends and neighbors, let it go to waste, or find a way to make it keep through the winter and spring.

Like you, friends and neighbors can use only so much produce. Letting it go to waste is not a solution most of us would want to choose. But finding a way to keep that produce for future use is what this book is all about. In this section, you'll learn how to can it.

The first thing to know about canning vegetables is that it can be done—simply, safely, and with results that are nutritious, good-tasting, and downright gratifying. The second thing to know is that there are dangers involved—you *must* use the right equipment and you *must* follow directions to the letter; anything less spells failure, and where home canning of low-acid foods (vegetables, meat, poultry, and fish) is concerned, failure can be fatal.

The only safe way to can these low-acid foods is in a steam pressure canner under specific amounts of pressure and for specific periods, as shown in the chart on pages 43–45.

At high elevations, pressure adjustments are necessary; these are indicated in a note at the top of the chart.

As a safety precaution, even the most carefully canned vegetables should be heated to a boil and then hard simmer (205° to 210°F) for 15 minutes before they're served.

Here are some ways *not* to can vegetables—they are all fraught with danger: Never process vegetables in a regular canning kettle, using the water bath method prescribed for canning fruits and tomatoes—the heat of this method is not sufficient to prevent dangerous spoilage in low-acid foods. Nor can the everyday "pressure cooker"—the one designed for fast cooking—be used for canning. Finally, never use the old-fashioned oven canning method; an oven provides a slow rate of heat transfer, as well as uneven heat distribution.

Equipment you'll need

The number one necessity is the steam pressure canner; you'll see one pictured on page 40. Jars and some sizable cooking utensils, plus a few accessories, are the only other items of equipment you need, beyond your kitchen range.

The steam pressure canner is a heavy kettle with a tight-fitting cover that can be locked down to make it steam-tight. The cover is fitted with a pressure gauge and a petcock vent with a safety valve.

Two types of canners are available—one has a weighted gauge, the other a dial.

The *weighted gauge* is simple and accurate, and it never needs calibrating. It automatically limits pressure by a control preset for 5, 10, or 15 pounds. With only one exception, all of our canning requires 10 pounds (240°F) pressure; the exception is bell peppers, which are processed at 5 pounds pressure.

The *dial control* on the other type of canner is a numbered instrument that indicates the pressure and temperature at which the jars of food are being processed. The instrument should be checked for accuracy every season—see the manufacturer's instructions or inquire at the store where you purchased the canner. In some areas, the Cooperative Extension Service is equipped to check these instruments.

If the checking indicates that your gauge is as much as 5 pounds off, replace the gauge. But if it's off by less than 5 pounds, you can compensate by adjusting the number of pounds of pressure at which you process your jars of vegetables.

(Continued on page 38)

GUARD AGAINST BOTULISM

If you've followed the guidelines for selecting and preparing vegetables, meats, poultry, and fish, and if you've processed them in a steam pressure canner *precisely* as directed, there's little or no chance of food spoilage.

Nevertheless, you should be aware that botulism, a deadly form of food spoilage, can occur in low-acid foods canned by any method except the steam pressure canner one—with directions followed to the letter. Low-acid foods include virtually all vegetables, meats, poultry, and fish. The exception is tomatoes, which are high in acid; though we think of them as vegetables, botanically they are fruits. Botulism rarely occurs in tomatoes and other fruits.

Botulism poisoning is caused by food that contains toxins produced by the bacterium *Clostridium botulinum*. It can be fatal. The spores are extremely resistant to heat, and they grow in jars of canned low-acid foods.

Symptoms of botulism poisoning usually begin within 12 to 36 hours after contaminated food is eaten. They include double vision, inability to swallow, and speech and respiratory difficulties. Medical treatment should be sought immediately; there are antitoxins.

Unfortunately, because this kind of spoilage can't be seen and sometimes has no odor, it's not easy to detect. But there are signs to watch for. **Do not even taste** foods from jars that show signs of gas pressure—a bulging lid, any oozing from under the lid, tiny upward-moving bubbles. Nor should you taste food that looks mushy or moldy or gives off a disagreeable odor when opened, or food from a jar whose lid shows signs of corrosion. (For the same reasons, of course, don't buy cans or jars of food that are swollen or leaking. Take them to the store manager as suspect, and contact local health authorities.)

The food from such jars should not just be thrown away or flushed down the toilet—it could contaminate the water supply. First boil the food for 10 minutes or longer to destroy the toxins; then flush down the toilet. Boil the jar, lid, and ring band in strong detergent and water, and then discard. Wash your hands—and anything else that might have come into contact with the contamination—in a bleach solution, and rinse thoroughly.

Innocent-looking jars of food can cause anxiety. What if the food and jar look perfectly normal, but you have some lurking doubt about how carefully you followed the directions? What if you bought some canned vegetables at a garage sale (probably not a good idea) and then got cold feet? Or what if Uncle Fred has taken up canning since he's retired, and he's eager to share the results?

Easy. Just heat the food as outlined in step 9 (at right).

Then you can taste it (the boiling will have destroyed any toxin) and eat it worry-free if it tastes all right. Of course, all the cooking will have taken its toll of the nutrients, flavor, and texture.

These canning cautions will help you guard against botulism:

1. Don't experiment or take short cuts in home canning. Use only tested, approved methods.

2. Use fresh, firm (not overripe), thoroughly washed vegetables and the freshest meats, poultry, and fish. Can vegetables as soon as possible after they're picked.

3. Use jars and lids made especially for home canning, and discard jars that are cracked or nicked.

4. Don't overpack foods. Trying to get too much food into a jar may result in underprocessing and spoilage.

5. Never use sealing lids a second time. Once the sealant on the lids has been through the processing stage, it is ineffective for sealing again, and therefore unsafe. Buy new lids.

6. Use only a steam pressure canner with an accurate gauge (have it tested annually). Process for the full required time, and at the correct temperature. Follow directions *exactly*, and make adjustments for high elevations (see Note, pages 43 and 69).

7. Test each jar's seal before storing.

8. Never use—or even taste—canned food that shows signs of spoilage.

9. For added safety, before serving any home canned vegetables (not tomatoes), meats, poultry, or fish, bring to a boil and then hard simmer (205° to 210° F) for 15 minutes.

If the gauge reads
 1 pound high—process at 11 pounds
 2 pounds high—process at 12 pounds
 3 pounds high—process at 13 pounds
 4 pounds high—process at 14 pounds
If the gauge reads
 1 pound low—process at 9 pounds
 2 pounds low—process at 8 pounds
 3 pounds low—process at 7 pounds
 4 pounds low—process at 6 pounds

Whether you use a weighted gauge or dial control canner, pay attention if steam starts escaping from under the lid, and replace the neoprene gasket before beginning your next canning project.

The steam pressure canner comes equipped with a rack that has lots of openings to allow the steam to circulate. The rack should be stable, so the jars won't tip or touch the bottom of the canner or touch other jars.

When you can in pint or half-pint jars, you may want to process two layers of jars at a time, if the canner can accommodate their combined height. Place a rack (a cake rack will do) on the tops of the jars in the first layer, and stagger the jars for the second layer so the steam can circulate all around.

Other equipment includes a large kettle or two for precooking vegetables and keeping jars hot, depending on the vegetables you're canning; for specifics, see the vegetable chart on pages 43–45.

Be sure you have enough jars on hand, and that they're in good condition, without cracks or chips. Ring bands can be used season after season, as long as they're not bent or corroded. Sealing lids, though, must be brand new—once a lid has been through the processing stage, the sealant is no longer effective.

It's a good idea to buy jars and lids before canning season begins, because it's not uncommon for stores to run out of them once the season is at full tilt.

Pictured on page 18 are some useful-to-necessary accessories for the home canner.

Step-by-step canning for vegetables

1 Read carefully all preceding information on canning vegetables, and check the vegetable chart (pages 43–45) for instructions for the particular vegetable you're about to can.

2 Get out steam pressure canner, jars (discard any that have nicks or cracks), lids (they must be new), ring bands, and other items listed under "Equipment you'll need" (page 36). Be sure all equipment is clean and ready to use. Scald lids in boiling water; keep in very hot water until time to use. Place jars in a kettle of very hot water.

3 Place pressure canner on range element, put rack into canner, and pour in hot water to a depth of 2 to 3 inches (enough to keep canner from boiling dry). Cover canner and turn on range element to medium-high to bring water to a boil; keep it hot while you prepare vegetables.

4 Following chart directions, prepare only enough vegetables for one canner load at a time. In deciding whether or not to precook (if chart offers a choice), consider that precooking makes it possible to pack more food into a jar; it also reduces likelihood of floating food.

To precook, use modest amount of water—cooking liquid holds lots of nutrients

Prepare enough vegetables for one canner load at a time

Tomato press issues seeded pulp from one side, juice from the other for garden-fresh marinara sauce to exhilarate your pasta dishes the whole year around. See page 94 for the recipe.

and you'll want to use all of it in filling jars; if you run short, you can use boiling water to complete filling of jars.

Most vegetables can be canned without salt if you prefer; artichokes, though, require an acid-brine solution as indicated in chart.

5 Remove a jar from hot water and fill with vegetable as instructed in chart—don't pack too tightly. Stand filled jar in very hot water (a regular canning kettle works nicely) and fill remaining jars one at a time. Pour in boiling cooking liquid, dividing it among jars; if necessary, add boiling water to fill jars to point indicated in chart; be sure to leave correct head space. Run a narrow spatula gently around each jar between food and jar sides, to release any air bubbles; add more liquid if necessary.

Don't pack jar too tightly

6 With a damp cloth, wipe jar rim clean (any food particles would prevent a seal). Lift a jar lid from hot water and place it on jar (if lids stick together, plunge into cold water, then hot). Screw ring band on by hand; don't overtighten. Repeat with remaining jars.

7 Turn heat to medium-high. Place jars on rack in canner, spaced so they don't touch canner sides or each other.

8 Before processing, you must vent pressure canner to eliminate all air inside. To do this, fasten down canner lid, leaving petcock open (or vent pipe uncovered) and let a jet of air escape for at least 10 minutes. (Air left in canner would prevent temperature from rising as high as necessary for canning, resulting in uneven heat distribution and possible spoilage.)

Let jet of steam escape for 10 minutes before closing petcock (or applying weighted gauge)

9 After venting canner, close petcock (or put on weighted gauge) and bring canner to required pressure level (see chart; check altitude note at top of chart if you are canning at elevation higher than 1,000 feet). Process for length of time indicated in chart, making sure pressure gauge never falls below required level—you'll have to watch gauge constantly and regulate heating element as necessary.

10 After processing, remove canner from heat to another range element—never to a cold surface. Canner will be heavy; be careful not to tilt it—toppled jars may not seal.

11 Let canner cool gradually—it will take about ½ hour; never try to speed the process under cold water. About 2 minutes after pressure has returned to zero on gauge, slowly open petcock (or remove weighted gauge).

12 Allow canner to cool for about 15 minutes after opening petcock. Then remove lid by opening canner away from you so you don't get steam in your face. Leave jars in canner 10 to 15 minutes longer—*do not disturb seal.*

Remove lid by opening canner away from you

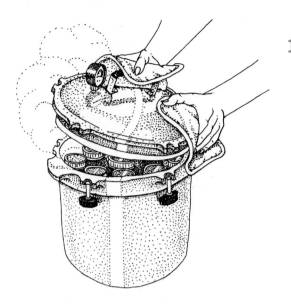

13 At end of cooling time, remove jars with a jar lifter. Set jars on a folded cloth or board—never on a cold surface. Leave enough room between jars for air to circulate. You'll notice bubbling going on in jars—this indicates they are properly sealed and contents are still boiling under vacuum.

Remove jars with jar lifter

When jars are cool, remove ring bands, if desired. (To loosen a band that sticks, cover with a hot, damp cloth for 1 to 2 minutes; then loosen.)

14 Test seal by pressing lid with your finger. If it stays down when pressed, jar is sealed; if lid pops back up, it is not sealed.

Test seal by pressing lid with your finger; it should stay down

If a jar hasn't sealed by the time it's cool, refrigerate and use food within a few days—if it looks and smells all right. Or if you want to recan it, be aware that much of the food value and flavor will be lost, since you must process the jar again for the full length of time. It will be safe to eat, though, if it seals on the second try. Use a new lid—a lid that's been through the processing stage won't seal.

15 If, for some reason, you didn't follow directions in every detail, be aware of food poisoning by reading the information on botulism (page 37) and following directions given.

16 Store jars in a cool, dark place.

17 For ultimate safety, some authorities recommend the following procedure for any home-canned, low-acid foods: before serving, bring to a boil and then hard simmer (205° to 210°F) for 15 minutes.

Guide for Canning Vegetables

NOTE: At elevations higher than 1,000 feet, increase pressure of steam pressure canner, adding 1 pound for elevations between 1,001 and 2,000 feet, and ½ pound for each additional 1,000 feet. Processing times remain the same.

Broccoli, Brussels sprouts, cabbage, cauliflower, cucumbers, eggplant, greens, parsnips, rutabagas, and spinach are not recommended for canning.

Vegetables	Quantity to yield 1 quart	How to prepare	Processing time at 10 pounds pressure Pints	Quarts
Artichoke hearts **Baby artichokes**	35 to 40 1¼-inch or 20 to 30 2-inch, trimmed whole artichokes	Cut off tops and stem, leaving 1¼" to 2". Trim outer leaves to nonfibrous heart. Precook for 5 minutes in boiling water to which you've added ¾ cup vinegar per gallon. Drain and discard cooking liquid. Pack hot artichoke hearts into hot jars, filling to neck. Cover with a boiling brine prepared by adding ¾ cup vinegar or lemon juice and 3 tablespoons salt to 1 gallon water. Fill, leaving ½" head space. Apply lid and ring band.	25 min.	25 min.
Asparagus	2¼ to 4½ lbs.	Wash and cut off scales (bracts). Cut stalks into lengths ¾" shorter than jar, or cut into 1" to 2" pieces. Blanch in boiling water for 1 to 3 minutes to wilt, then plunge into cold water until cool enough to handle. For whole pack, gather a bundle of stalks with cut ends down and pack (not too tightly) into jars; or fill to neck of jars with cut pieces. Add salt (½ teaspoon for pints, 1 teaspoon for quarts); then add boiling cooking liquid or water to cover asparagus leaving ½" head space. Apply lid and ring band.	28 min.	32 min.
Beans, green	1½ to 2½ lbs.	Wash; string if necessary. Leave whole or cut into 1" to 1½" pieces.		
		To pack hot, precook in boiling water until pliable (2 to 5 minutes). Pack hot beans into hot jars, standing whole beans on ends or packing cut beans up to jar shoulder. Add salt (½ teaspoon for pint jars, 1 teaspoon for quarts); then add boiling cooking liquid or water to cover beans, leaving ½" to ¾" head space. Apply lid and ring band.	25 min.	30 min.
		To pack raw, use pieces cut no larger than 1". Pack tightly into jars up to jar shoulders; follow remaining directions above.	20 min.	25 min.
Beans, lima	3 to 5 lbs.	Hull and rinse beans.		
		To pack hot, precook in a small amount of boiling water until skins wrinkle (1 to 4 minutes). Pack hot beans loosely into hot jars to within 1" of pint jar tops (1½" for quarts). Add salt (½ teaspoon for pints, 1 teaspoon for quarts); then add boiling cooking liquid or water to cover beans, leaving ½" to ¾" head space. Apply lid and ring band. **To pack raw,** omit precooking; follow remaining directions above.	40 min.	50 min.

(Continued on next page)

Pantry plenty means jar upon jar of assorted good tastes. Top shelf (left to right): green beans, apricot halves, fresh refrigerator pickles (recipe on page 56), plums. Middle shelf: giardiniera (recipe on page 55), mushrooms, baby corn, carrots, and corn. Bottom shelf: peach halves, quick dill pickles (recipe on page 50), tomatoes, and peas. For canning instructions, see charts on pages 10–11 (fruits) and pages 43–45 (vegetables).

Vegetables	Quantity to yield 1 quart	How to prepare	Processing time at 10 pounds pressure Pints	Quarts
Beets	2½ to 3½ lbs.	Scrub, don't peel. Leave on roots and 1″ to 1½″ of tops. Boil until skins slip off (about 15 minutes). Dip in cold water. Peel, trim, and slice ¼″ thick. Discard woody beets. Reheat in small amount of water. Pack hot beets into hot jars, filling jars to shoulders. Add salt (½ teaspoon to pints, 1 teaspoon to quarts); then add boiling liquid in which beets were reheated; add boiling water if needed to cover beets, leaving ½″ head space. Apply lid and ring band.	35 min.	40 min.
Carrots	2 to 3 lbs.	Wash and scrape. Slice, or cut into sticks that are 1″ shorter than jars. Pack slices into jars up to shoulder, or arrange sticks upright in jars to within 1″ of top. Add salt (½ teaspoon to pints, 1 teaspoon to quarts); then add boiling water to cover carrots, allowing ½″ to ¾″ head space. Apply lids and ring bands.	30 min.	30 min.
Celery	1½ to 2½ lbs.	Wash; remove leafy tops and coarse strings. Slice, or cut into lengths ¾″ to 1″ shorter than jars. **To pack hot,** use sliced celery; precook for 1 to 3 minutes, until crisp-tender. Pack hot celery into hot jars up to jar shoulders. Add salt (½ teaspoon to pints, 1 teaspoon to quarts); then add boiling cooking liquid or water, leaving about ½″ head space. Apply lids and ring bands.	35 min.	35 min.
		To pack raw, pack slices loosely up to jar shoulder or arrange long pieces upright in jars. Proceed as directed for hot pack.	30 min.	30 min.
Corn	3 to 6 lbs. (8 to 16 ears)	Remove husks and silk. **For whole kernel corn,** use a sharp knife to cut raw kernels from cob ⅔ of total depth. Do not scrape cobs. In a pan, cover corn with brine made by adding 1 tablespoon salt to each quart water. Heat to boiling and pack hot into hot jars to within 1″ of tops. Then add boiling brine, leaving 1″ head space. Apply lids and ring bands.	55 min.	70 min.
		For cream-style corn, cut corn off cob as for whole kernel corn, then scrape cobs, being careful not to scrape off any of the cob material. NOTE: Don't use quart jars—processing time would be too long. In a pan, cover corn with brine made from ½ teaspoon salt to each pint of water; proceed as for whole kernel corn; leave 1¼″ head space in pint jars when packed with mixture of corn and brine. Apply lids and ring bands. **For whole miniature corn,** pickling is recommended.	85 min.	—
Mushrooms	1½ lbs.	NOTE: Don't use quart jars—mushrooms would become overcooked in processing. Trim stems and discolored parts. Soak in cold water for 10 minutes, then wash. Leave small mushrooms whole; cut larger ones into halves or quarters. Place in a steamer over boiling water and steam for 4 minutes; or heat gently for 15 minutes in a covered pan without liquid. Pack hot mushrooms into hot jars to jar shoulders. Add ½ teaspoon salt to pints. Add boiling cooking liquid or water to cover mushrooms, leaving ½″ head space at top (don't use quart jars). Apply lids and ring bands.	30 min.	—
Onions small white		To peel, pour boiling water over onions, let stand 2 to 3 minutes, then drain and peel. Precook for 5 minutes in boiling water to which you've added ¾ cup vinegar per gallon. Drain, saving cooking liquid. Pack hot into hot jars to jar shoulders. Cover with cooking liquid to which you've added 3 tablespoons salt per gallon. Leave ½″ head space. Apply lids and ring bands.	25 min.	5 min.

Vegetables	Quantity to yield 1 quart	How to prepare	Processing time at 10 pounds pressure Pints	Quarts
Peas	3 to 6 lbs.	Shell and wash, using tender, young peas. **To pack hot,** precook in a small amount of water for 1 to 4 minutes or until skins wrinkle. Pack hot into hot jars to within 1¼" of tops. Add ½ teaspoon salt to pints; 1 teaspoon salt to quarts. Cover with boiling cooking liquid; add boiling water if needed leaving 1" head space. Apply lids and ring bands.	40 min.	45 min.
		To pack raw, pack loosely to within 1" of jar tops. Add salt as for hot pack. Cover with boiling water, leaving ¾" head space. Apply lids and ring bands.	40 min.	45 min.
Peppers, bell (green and red)	2 to 3 lbs.	Wash. Cut out stem end of each pepper and remove core and seeds. Place in a shallow pan in a 400° oven until skins are slightly scorched and separate. Plunge into cold water and peel. Pack cooled peppers loosely into jars to jar shoulders. Add ½ teaspoon salt and 1 tablespoon lemon juice to pints, 1 teaspoon salt and 1 tablespoon lemon juice to quarts. Cover with boiling water, leaving ½" head space. Apply lids and ring bands. **Process peppers** at only 5 pounds pressure, as higher pressures affect texture and flavor. Process pints for 50 minutes, quarts for 60 minutes.	See information below left	
Potatoes, new Other potatoes not recommended for canning	4 to 6 lbs.	Scrape peel off new potatoes. Leave small ones whole; cut larger ones into halves. Pack raw into jars to jar shoulders. Pour over boiling brine made by adding 1½ to 2 tablespoons salt to 1 quart water, leaving ½" head space. Apply lids and ring bands.	35 min.	40 min.
Potatoes, sweet	2 to 3 lbs.	Wash and remove any blemishes. **To pack dry,** place in steamer over boiling water or boil in a small amount of water until crisp-tender. Peel and cut into pieces if large. Pack tightly into jars, pressing to fill spaces. Add no salt or liquid. Apply lids and ring bands.	65 min.	95 min.
		To pack wet, steam or boil as for dry pack; but remove as soon as skins slip off easily. Peel, cut into pieces, and pack hot into jars to within 1" of tops. Add ½ teaspoon salt to quarts. Cover with boiling water or a medium syrup (see Syrups on page 7), leaving ¾" head space. Apply lids and ring bands.	55 min.	90 min.
Squash, summer crookneck, zucchini, pattypan	1½ lbs.	Wash and trim ends, don't peel. Cut into ½"-thick slices. **To pack hot,** put into a pan, add water to just cover, and bring to boiling. Pack hot into hot jars, filling loosely up to jar shoulders. Add ½ teaspoon salt to pints, 1 teaspoon to quarts. Cover with boiling cooking liquid, leaving ½" head space. Apply lids and ring bands.	30 min.	40 min.
		To pack raw, pack slices tightly into jars to within 1" of tops. Add salt as for hot pack, then fill jars with boiling water, leaving ½" head space. Apply lids and ring bands.	25 min.	30 min.
Squash, winter banana, butternut, Hubbard, pumpkin	1½ to 3 lbs.	Cut into 1" by 3" strips, scraping out all fibrous material and seeds. Place in a steamer over boiling water or boil in a small amount of water until soft. Scrape pulp from rind and press through a colander, or mash. Put into a pan and bring to a boil, stirring. Pack hot into hot jars to within ½" to ¾" of tops. Add ½ teaspoon salt to pints, 1 teaspoon to quarts. Apply lids and ring bands.	85 min.	115 min.
Tomatoes (see under Guide for Canning Fruit on page 11)				
Turnips	2 to 3 lbs.	Wash and peel or scrape. Cut in uniform ¼"-thick slices or about ½" dice. Pack raw into jars, filling up to jar shoulders. Add ½ teaspoon salt to pints, 1 teaspoon to quarts. Pour in boiling water to cover, leaving ½" to ¾" head space. Apply lids and ring bands.	30 min.	30 min.

Vegetable Recipes

Seasoned Tomato Paste

Making your own tomato paste is an economical way to "put up" tomatoes. Use this seasoned paste for any recipe that calls for canned tomato paste.

- 15 **pounds fully ripe tomatoes, coarsely chopped (about 8 quarts)**
- 4 **large red or green bell peppers, seeded and coarsely chopped**
- 3 **medium-size onions, coarsely chopped**
- 4 **meduim-size carrots, coarsely chopped**
- 2 or 3 **cloves garlic, coarsely chopped**

In a blender or food processor, whirl tomatoes, peppers, onions, carrots, and garlic, a small amount at a time, until smooth. Press through a wire strainer and discard pulp.

In a 12-quart pot, bring purée to boiling over medium-high heat. Boil gently, uncovered and stirring occasionally, for about 5 hours or until thick enough to mound on a spoon. As mixture thickens, stir often, reduce heat, and partially cover.

Prepare 5 pint-size canning jars, following step 2 on page 8. Then proceed with steps 3 and 5–13, filling jars to within ¼ inch of rim. Process for 30 minutes. Makes 5 pints.

Spicy Tomato Catsup

Making homemade catsup is an easy way to use an overabundance of tomatoes. A blender or food processor is most helpful.

- 12 **pounds ripe tomatoes, coarsely chopped**
- 2 **large onions, cut into pieces**
- 1 **red bell pepper, seeded and cut into pieces**
- 1 **tablespoon** *each* **mustard seed, whole black peppers, and dry basil**
- 2 **teaspoons whole allspice**
- 2 **small dried hot chile peppers**
- 1 **large bay leaf**
- 1 **whole cinnamon stick**
- 1½ **cups firmly packed brown sugar**
- 1 **tablespoon** *each* **salt and paprika**
- 1 **cup vinegar**

In a blender or food processor, whirl tomatoes, onions, and bell pepper, a small amount at a time, until smooth. Press through a wire strainer and discard pulp. You should have 6 quarts of purée.

In an 8 to 10-quart pot, bring purée to boiling over medium-high heat. Boil gently, uncovered and stirring often, until reduced by about half (about 1 hour).

Into a looosely tied cheesecloth bag, place mustard seed, black peppers, basil, allspice, hot chile peppers, bay leaf, and cinnamon stick. Add to purée. Stir in brown sugar, salt, and paprika until well blended. Continue cooking over medium-high heat until very thick (about 1½ to 2 hours).

As mixture thickens, stir often and reduce heat to prevent sticking. Add vinegar during last 10 to 15 minutes of cooking. Discard spice bag.

You can chill the catsup, pour into freezer containers, cover, and freeze, if you like.

Or prepare 4 pint-size canning jars, following step 2 on page 8. Then proceed with steps 3 and 5–13, filling jars to within ¼ inch of rim. Process for 20 minutes. Makes 2 quarts.

Hot & Spicy Chile Sauce

Serve this sauce spooned onto hot dogs, hamburgers, or steaks.

- 4 to 5 **pounds ripe tomatoes**
- 1 **large onion, chopped**
- ¾ **cup sugar**
- 1¼ **cups cider vinegar**
- 1 **teaspoon crushed red pepper (seeds removed)**
- 1 **teaspoon** *each* **mustard seed and salt**
- ½ **teaspoon** *each* **ground ginger and nutmeg**
- ¼ **teaspoon curry powder**

Peel, core, and coarsely chop tomatoes; you should have 8 cups. In a heavy 5-quart pot, combine tomatoes, onion, sugar, vinegar, red pepper, mustard seed, salt, ginger, nutmeg, and curry powder. Bring to a boil over medium-high heat; then reduce heat and simmer, uncovered and stirring often as mixture thickens, until reduced to about 2 pints (about 2 hours).

Meanwhile, prepare 2 pint-size canning jars, following step 2 on page 8. Then proceed, following steps 3 and 5–13, filling jars to within ⅛ of rim. Process for 15 minutes. Makes 2 pints.

Antipasto parade encircles tuna garnished with anchovies and capers, presented with rolled salami and wedges of Brie. Extra delicacies (clockwise from upper left): artichoke hearts (page 43), carrots (chart, page 44), mushrooms (chart, page 44), giardiniera (page 55), caponata (page 94), purchased olives and peppers, hard-cooked egg quarters, and celery.

PICKLING FRUITS & VEGETABLES

Whether you're an experienced hand at pickling fruits and vegetables, or a novice considering putting up your first batch, you'll appreciate the easy pickle-making procedures in this section. It includes recipes for a quick dill and a variety of sweet pickles, as well as pickled vegetables, fruits, relishes, and chutneys.

Pickling generally applies to the method of preserving any food in a brine or vinegar. This includes vegetables, fruits, relishes, and chutneys.

Pickles are usually cucumbers that have been preserved in a brine or vinegar.

Relishes are piquant blends of vegetables, fruits, spices, and vinegar. They are tasty accompaniments to any number of meats, but too often they're served only with hot dogs and hamburgers.

Chutneys are a type of relish, too, varying from hot and spicy to mild and tangy. Though usually associated with Middle Eastern or Indian food, they can be served as a condiment complementing a wide range of foods.

Important ingredients

Cucumbers —in fact all fruits and all vegetables—should be firm, fresh, free of blemishes, and well washed. You'll want to preserve them as soon as possible to ensure their freshness. Small to medium cucumbers may be left whole; larger cucumbers should be sliced or cut into chunks. A regular cucumber has fewer spines than the pickling cucumber; it's also darker and larger.

Any table salt but preferably the noniodized variety may be used in pickling. Do not use a salt substitute.

Vinegar should be clear and free of sediment, with 4 to 5 percent acetic acid. Do not use homemade vinegar; it may not be acetic enough. Distilled white vinegar best preserves the color in foods. Cider vinegar can cause darkening of the food but may be preferred for its flavor and aroma. (Avoid long boiling of vinegar; boiling depletes the acetic acid, so important in making pickles.)

Fresh herbs and spices give the best flavor. Dill, garlic, and tarragon are frequently used.

Sugar should be granulated cane or beet sugar. Brown sugar tends to darken the color and gives a strong flavor.

Water with a high iron content may also cause darkening.

Equipment you'll need

The most important piece of equipment for pickling is a pot large enough to hold all your ingredients so they won't boil over the top as they cook. Use only aluminum, stainless steel, enamelware, or glass utensils. Copper may turn pickles an unappetizing shade of off-green; iron turns them black. *Caution: Never use galvanized containers for pickling*—the action of acid or salt with zinc can develop a poisonous substance.

A canning kettle is necessary if you plan to process your jars in one. Even if you're not planning to use one for processing, it's ideal for sterilizing jars. You'll need a small pan for sterilizing lids.

Pickles should be processed at a simmering temperature of 170°–180°F—no higher and no lower. So a cooking thermometer is useful for testing the temperature of the simmering water.

Be sure you have enough jars on hand, and that they're in good condition, without cracks or chips. Ring bands can be used season after season, as long as they're not bent or corroded. Sealing lids, though, must be brand new—once a lid

has been through the processing stage, the sealant is no longer effective.

It's a good idea to buy jars and lids before canning season begins, because it's not uncommon for stores to run out of them once the season is at full tilt.

Pictured on page 18 are some useful-to-necessary accessories for the home canner.

Step-by-step canning for pickles, relishes, & chutneys

Some pickled foods with a high acid content, such as pickles and relishes, may be canned without a canning kettle—you simply put boiling hot food into hot, sterilized jars. Other pickled foods, such as chutneys, are more subject to spoilage and must be processed in their jars in a canning kettle for a specified length of time.

Even though a recipe calls for processing without a canning kettle, you can, if you prefer, process with a canning kettle for 20 minutes at simmering temperatures (170°–180°F; use a thermometer to check). This processing helps to assure a seal and thus reduces the chance of spoilage.

Processing without a Canning Kettle

1 Get out canning jars, lids (they must be new), and ring bands. Discard nicked or cracked jars (see illustration, page 8) and any rusted, bent, or corroded ring bands. Immerse jars in boiling water and keep them immersed until ready to fill. Immerse lids in a small pan of boiling water until ready to use.

2 In a large pot, heat food to boiling as described in recipe.

3 Fill one hot jar at a time with boiling hot food. Fill to top of jar or to within head space called for in recipe.

4 With a damp cloth, wipe jar rim clean. Place lid on jar and screw on ring band as tightly as you comfortably can.

5 Set jars on a folded towel away from drafts; let cool. Leave on ring bands until jars are cool.

6 Test seal by pressing lid with your finger. If it stays down when pressed, jar is sealed. If it pops back up, it's not sealed. Store any unsealed jars in the refrigerator and use within a month. Store sealed jars in a cool, dry place. Refrigerate after opening.

Processing with a Canning Kettle (Water Bath Method)

1 Get out canning kettle, jars, lids, ring bands, and any other accessories you might need (see page 5). Discard nicked or cracked jars (see illustration, page 8) and any rusted, bent, or corroded ring bands. Canning jars and lids should be clean and hot. A dishwasher is ideal for both washing and keeping jars hot. If you don't have a dishwasher, wash jars, then fill them with hot water until ready to fill with food. Immerse lids in boiling water until ready to use.

2 In a large pot, heat food to boiling as described in recipe.

3 Place rack in canning kettle and fill kettle about half full with hot water. Place kettle, covered, on range to heat. In a large teakettle or pan, heat additional water to add later.

4 Fill hot jars, one at a time, with boiling hot food. Fill to within ¼ inch of rim for pint and half-pint jars, to within ½ inch of rim for quart jars, unless stated otherwise in recipe.

5 Run a narrow spatula down between food and jar to release air bubbles. Fill with more cooking liquid, if necessary.

6 With a damp cloth, wipe jar rim clean (any food particles would prevent a seal). Place lids on jars and screw on ring bands as tightly as you comfortably can.

7 Put jars on rack in canning kettle, making sure they don't touch kettle's sides or each other. Add hot water if necessary—water must cover jar lids by 1 to 2 inches (see illustration, page 9). Bring to simmering (170°–180°F; use a thermometer to check) and keep water simmering throughout processing time specified in recipe. (Begin counting processing time when water begins to simmer.)

(Continued on next page)

8 At end of processing time, take jars out of water with a jar lifter. Don't disturb seal.

9 Set jars on a folded towel away from drafts; let cool. Leave on ring bands until jars are cool.

10 Test seal by pressing lid with your finger. If it stays down when pressed, jar is sealed. If it pops back up, it's not sealed. Store any unsealed jars in the refrigerator and use within a month. Label and store sealed jars in a cool, dry place. Refrigerate after opening.

Pickle, Relish & Chutney Recipes

Quick Dill Pickles

(Pictured on page 42)

A favorite for generations, this old-fashioned dill pickle recipe also comes with a variation for kosher-style dills.

- 4 **pounds cucumbers (unpeeled)**
- 3 **tablespoons salt**
- 3 **cups** *each* **vinegar and water**
- 1 **tablespoon whole mixed pickling spice**
- 18 **whole black peppers**
- 9 **heads (tops) fresh dill or 3 tablespoons dill seed**

Prepare 6 pint-size or 3 quart-size canning jars, following step 1 under "Processing with a Canning Kettle," page 49.

If using larger than 4-inch cucumbers, slice, quarter, or halve lengthwise. In a large pot or pan, combine salt, vinegar, and water. Bring to a boil.

Pack cucumbers into clean, hot jars. For each quart jar, add 1 teaspoon pickling spice, 6 whole black peppers, and 3 heads (tops) fresh dill or 1 tablespoon dill seed. For each pint jar, add ½ teaspoon pickling spice, 3 whole black peppers, and 1½ heads (tops) fresh dill or 1½ teaspoons dill seed.

Fill jars with boiling vinegar-salt solution to ½ inch from top of quart jars or ¼ inch from top of pint jars. Proceed with steps 4–10 under "Processing with a Canning Kettle," page 49. Process 4-inch-size whole cucumbers for 20 minutes in quart jars, 10 minutes in pint jars. Process smaller whole cucumbers, as well as slices, halves, or quarters, for 7 minutes in quart jars, 5 minutes in pint jars. Makes 6 pints.

Kosher-style dill pickles. Follow recipe for quick dill pickles, but add 2 cloves **garlic** (peeled and halved) to each jar.

Mixed Sweet Cucumber Pickles

Commonly called bread-and-butter pickles, these spicy sweet slices of cucumbers and vegetables soak in a salt water solution for extra crispness and crunch.

- 4 **large green peppers**
- 4 **pounds onions**
- 10 **pounds cucumbers (unpeeled), sliced ¼ inch thick**
- ½ **cup salt**
   Ice water
- 5 **cups** *each* **white wine vinegar and sugar**
- 1 **cup water**
- 2 **tablespoons** *each* **mustard seed and celery seed**
- 1 **teaspoon turmeric**
- ½ **teaspoon ground cloves**

Remove and discard stems and seeds from peppers. Cut peppers into 1-inch squares. Cut onions into 1-inch cubes and place in an 8 to 10-quart pot along with peppers and sliced cucumbers. Sprinkle with salt and cover with ice water; stir to blend well. Let stand for 3 hours, stirring occasionally. Drain thoroughly.

Prepare 7 or 8 quart-size canning jars and lids, following step 1 under "Processing without a Canning Kettle," page 49.

In the same large pot, combine vinegar, sugar, water, mustard seed, celery seed, turmeric, and cloves. Bring to a boil, uncovered, over high heat. Add half the drained vegetables. Reduce heat and simmer uncovered, stirring often, for 3 to 5 minutes.

With a slotted spoon, ladle vegetables into clean, hot canning jars, packing vegetables firmly so jars are well filled. Fill each jar with hot pickling liquid to within ⅛ inch of rim. Reheat remaining pickling liquid to boiling, add remaining vegetables, and simmer as directed above. Fill remaining jars with vegetables and pickling liquid as directed above.

Proceed with steps 4–9 under "Processing without a Canning Kettle," page 49. Makes 7 or 8 quarts.

Green Tomato Refrigerator Pickles

Garden-green tomatoes mix with other vegetables to make an unusual pickle you can serve with a meal or for a snack. The firm texture of green (unripe) tomatoes makes them a good choice for pickling.

10 to 12 medium-size green tomatoes
 2 medium-size onions
1 or 2 red or green bell peppers
3 or 4 large carrots
2 or 3 stalks celery
 7½ cups water
 2½ cups white vinegar
 4 tablespoons salt
 3 large cloves garlic, peeled and quartered
 3 small dried hot chili peppers, broken in half
 3 teaspoons mixed pickling spice

Prepare 3 quart-size canning jars, following step 1 under "Processing without a Canning Kettle," page 49.

Core tomatoes, cut into 6 to 8 wedges, and place in a bowl. Cut onions into 1-inch cubes and bell peppers into 1-inch squares; add to bowl. Cut carrots in half lengthwise, then cut carrots and celery into 1½-inch lengths; add to bowl. Mix vegetables thoroughly and set aside.

Heat water, vinegar, and salt to boiling; keep hot. Divide vegetables among jars. To each jar, add 4 garlic pieces, 2 pieces of chili pepper, and 1 teaspoon pickling spice. Quickly pour liquid into jars, filling to within ⅛ inch of rim.

Proceed with steps 4–6 under "Processing without a Canning Kettle," page 49. Makes 3 quarts.

Bread & Butter Slices

Cooked briefly in a spicy mustard syrup, these refrigerator pickles are less sweet than the seven-day variety.

2½ cups sugar
 2 cups cider vinegar
 1 cup water
 1 teaspoon *each* salt and celery seed
 1 tablespoon mustard seed
1½ tablespoons whole mixed pickling spice
3½ pounds medium-size cucumbers (unpeeled), sliced ¼ inch thick

Prepare 5 pint-size canning jars, following step 1 under "Processing without a Canner," page 49.

In a 5-quart pot, combine sugar, vinegar, water, salt, celery seed, mustard seed, and pickling spice. Bring to a boil, stirring to dissolve sugar. Add cucumber slices to syrup. Return mixture to a boil, turning cucumbers gently to coat with syrup. Continue boiling for 1½ minutes; remove from heat. Then proceed with steps 3–6 under "Processing without a Canning Kettle," page 49; filling to within ⅛ inch of rim. Makes 5 pints.

Spicy Seven-day Pickles

The pickling process in this recipe takes seven days, but it's so easy you'll want to try it. The pickles have a sweet taste similar to pickled watermelon rind.

3½ pounds medium-size cucumbers (unpeeled)
 4 cups sugar
 2 cups white vinegar
 1 tablespoon whole mixed pickling spice
 2 teaspoons salt

Place cucumbers in a deep bowl, cover them with boiling water, and let stand overnight. Repeat the process on the third and fourth days. On the fifth day, cut cucumbers into ¼-inch-thick slices and place in a clean, deep bowl.

In a 3-quart pot, combine sugar, vinegar, pickling spice, and salt. Bring to a boil to dissolve sugar; pour over cucumbers. Cool, cover bowl, and refrigerate for 2 days.

On the seventh day, prepare 5 pint-size canning jars, following step 1 under "Processing without a Canning Kettle," page 49. Bring cucumbers and vinegar solution to a boil. Then proceed with steps 3–6, filling to within ⅛ inch of rim. Makes 5 pints.

Ripening and tumbling to the ground each fall, olives in home gardens sometimes seem unfit for anything but dyeing pavement the color of a crude-oil spill. But in California and across the Southwest, where olive trees thrive, these same trees can produce a marvelous homemade delicacy. And if your own garden doesn't have a tree, perhaps a neighbor's property, nearby campus, or city street does; ask if you can remove the fruit.

Picking olives. Try to avoid bruising or skinning the fruit as you gather it off the tree. Suggested containers are a basket, a pail of water, or an old pillowcase. If you can't start the curing process within a day after picking, place fruit in a brine made of ¾ cup salt and 1 gallon water. You can let the fruit stand in a cool, well-ventilated place for up to four days.

Straight off the tree, olives taste unbelievably bitter. Curing takes care of that and gives the fruit its distinctive flavor. To produce green ripe olives we suggest a lye-and-brine process. The steps are straightforward, but you must follow directions patiently and carefully. Be sure to go through every step of the lye-curing, rinsing, and brining process. *Note: Olives may be cured at home, but don't try to can them. Improperly handled, olives can be a dangerous source of food poisoning.*

Green ripe olives are the result of a two-step lye-and-brine process that takes about two weeks. You get smooth, succulent olives with a slightly salty taste. Once cured, these olives lend themselves to several flavor variations. You can store them in the refrigerator or at room temperature for up to six months.

Serve your olives as you would serve commercially processed olives. For more prominent play, present them as the star of a simple but substantial appetizer with breads and cheeses.

Lye-cured Green Ripe Olives

Pick olives that are light green, pale straw color, or rosy red. Black fruit will get too soft when cured. You can use the lye-curing process with any of these varieties of olives: 'Ascolano', 'Manzanillo', 'Mission', and 'Sevillano'.

Start processing the olives early in the day, as the first steps take at least 12 hours and you must check the progress of the fruit frequently. For each 2 gallons of olives, you will need:

• one large container (at least 10 to 12 quarts), such as a stoneware crock, glass bowl, or plastic pail (do not use aluminum or galvanized metal)

• heavy-duty rubber gloves

• a long-handled wooden or stainless steel spoon

• household lye (from the supermarket)

• salt

• clean muslin cloths such as old dishtowels to keep fruit covered in the crock.

Sort through olives, discard any that are bruised, and measure fruit by the gallon. In a bowl, prepare a solution of 1 cup vinegar and 1 cup water. Keep it nearby to wash your skin in case of lye burn.

Lye-curing process. Allowing 1 gallon of water to cover each 2 gallons of fruit, place water in the crock. Using the rubber gloves to protect your hands, measure ¼ cup (2 oz.) lye for each gallon of water. Slowly pour lye into the water, stirring continuously with the long-handled spoon until lye dissolves. The lye heats the solution—allow it to cool for 30 minutes before adding olives. *(Do not pour lye in before you add water. Do not taste olives at any time during the lye-curing process.)*

Before you add the fruit, cut open a few fresh-picked olives so you'll know what the uncured flesh of olives looks like. Then you'll have a basis for comparison when you check for lye penetration.

Slowly pour in the olives; be very careful not to splash the lye solution. Crumple the cloth down into the solution on top of olives to keep them submerged. Exposure to air will cause fruit to oxidize and darken. (Commercial black ripe olives are green olives oxidized by a special process.)

Let stand, covered, where the temperature is 60° to 70°. Stir every 2 to 3 hours. After 6 hours, drain olives and set aside in another container. In the first container, prepare a fresh lye solution using the same proportions of water and lye as before. Return olives to the container with the new solution. Let stand for 6 hours.

Olives must remain in the solution until lye has penetrated to the pit in order to remove bitterness. To check lye penetration, cut two or three olives of varying size in half; *wear gloves.* Penetrated flesh will have turned a dark yellow green; unpenetrated flesh closer to the pit will be a lighter color. This process takes at least 12 hours, but can take as long as 30 hours, depending on the variety, maturity, and size of the olives.

If lye penetration is not complete after 12 hours, prepare a fresh lye solution following preceding directions. Let olives stand in solution until penetration has occurred; if convenient, stir and check every few hours, but there's no harm in letting them stand overnight without stirring or checking. If necessary, change lye solution again after 12 hours. As soon as most of the olives have been completely penetrated you can proceed to the next step. A few of the larger olives may not be quite finished, but they'll be sufficiently cured by this time to use with the rest.

Rinsing process. When lye penetration is complete, pour off lye solution and cover the olives with fresh cold water, taking care to keep fruit submerged with a clean cloth. Cover crock and let stand for 6 to 12 hours or overnight. Thereafter, change the water once a day until the color of the drained water has changed from a dark red to a light pink (about four to seven days).

Brining process. Allowing 1 gallon of water for each 2 gallons of olives, prepare a weak brine solution, using ½ cup regular table salt for each gallon of water. Stir until salt is dissolved. Slowly pour olives into brine. Cover container and let stand for 12 hours (olives will float initially). Drain off brine and prepare a second solution, using the same proportions of salt and water. Let olives stand, covered, for one week.

You can now eat the olives. If they are too salty, remove from brine the amount you wish to use within the next 3 days and cover with fresh water for 30 to 60 minutes, then drain and serve.

For the remaining olives, replace the brine with a stronger holding solution of 1¼ cups (1 lb.) table salt for each gallon of water. You can keep them for six months in the refrigerator, covered; replace the holding solution after four months. (To store large quantities of olives at room temperature, the University of California Agricultural Extension recommends placing the fruit in a holding solution of 2¼ cups salt for each gallon of water. Store, covered, up to six months.)

To reduce saltiness before eating, soak olives overnight or longer in fresh water. Drain and serve; refrigerate leftover drained olives and use within three days.

If at any time olives become mushy, moldy, or bad smelling, they should be discarded. Do not taste them.

Flavorings for Green Ripe Olives

For variety, you can add herbs and other seasonings to small quantities of olives packed in holding solution. For each quart of olives, you'll need about 2 cups (either strength) of brine holding solution. Select from seasoning ingredients as suggested below and stir into brine. Pack olives loosely into a quart jar, then pour seasoned brine over them. Cover and store in the refrigerator for at least five days for the olives to absorb flavors, or for as long as two months. To reduce saltiness before eating, soak in fresh water as previously directed.

Oregano: add ½ teaspoon oregano leaves, 4 whole black peppers, and 6 to 8 whole peeled garlic cloves to 2 cups brine.

Smoked: add 1 teaspoon liquid smoke to 2 cups brine.

Garlic: add 6 to 8 whole peeled garlic cloves to 2 cups brine.

Onion and tarragon: add 1 medium-size onion (sliced) and 1½ teaspoons tarragon to 2 cups brine.

Red wine and garlic: add 6 whole peeled garlic cloves and ½ cup red wine to 1½ cups brine.

Hot paprika: add 5 small dried hot chili peppers, 6 whole peeled garlic cloves, and 1 tablespoon paprika to 2 cups brine.

Pickled Artichokes

When fresh artichokes are plentiful in the markets, you might consider pickling the smaller ones (sometimes called hearts). After you pickle them, let them stand for 2 to 4 weeks. Then you can serve them as is, or marinate them.

To marinate, drain and mix artichokes with an oil (preferably olive oil) and vinegar dressing; then sprinkle with freshly minced parsley.

> **About 6½ dozen artichokes,** *each* **about 2 by 3 inches (not measuring stem)**
>
> **Acidified water (½ cup vinegar to** *each* **quart water)**
>
> 3 **quarts water**
>
> 3 **cups white wine vinegar**
>
> 4½ **teaspoons salt**
>
> 6 **medium-size or 12 small dried hot chili peppers**
>
> 6 **medium-size or 12 small cloves garlic**
>
> **About ¾ cup minced parsley (optional)**

Trim artichokes by cutting off stem and top ⅓ of each artichoke. Then break off all coarse bracts clear down to the very tender yellowish inner bracts. Trim stem end to make cone shape without cutting away any more of the bottom than necessary. Drop immediately into enough acidified water to cover. Keep artichokes immersed as much as possible by floating a pan lid or inverted plastic plate on the water. (Even if some artichokes darken from exposure to air, they will lighten when cooked.)

When all artichokes are trimmed, combine the 3 quarts water, the 3 cups wine vinegar, and salt in a large pot (not cast iron—it blackens artichokes) and bring to a boil. Drain artichokes of

acidified water and add them to vinegar solution; return to a boil. Reduce heat and simmer, uncovered, until barely tender (about 10 minutes).

Meanwhile, prepare 6 pint-size or 12 half-pint wide mouth canning jars, following step 1 under "Processing without a Canning Kettle," page 49.

With a slotted spoon, lift hot artichokes from vinegar solution and arrange in hot, sterilized jars; a pint will hold 12 to 13 artichokes, a half-pint 6 or 7. To each pint, add 1 medium-size chili pepper, 1 medium clove garlic, and 2 tablespoons parsley (if you wish). To each half pint, add 1 small chile, 1 small clove garlic, and 1 table-spoon parsley. Bring cooking liquid to a boil and pour into jars to cover artichokes, filling to within ¼ inch of rim. Proceed with steps 4–6 under "Processing without a Canning Kettle," page 49. Store in a cool, dark place for 2 to 4 weeks before using. Makes 6 pints or 12 half pints.

Miniature Pickled Onions

(Pictured on page 34)

The English serve these whole, small pickled onions as appetizers. The tart marinade cuts the heat of the raw onions and adds a spicy, piquant flavor. The smaller the onions, the better. If you use boiling onions larger than about ¾ inch in diameter, cut them in quarters to serve.

½ **cup salt**

3 **cups cold water**

2 **pounds small white boiling onions, peeled**

2 **cups white vinegar**

¼ **cup firmly packed brown sugar**

1 **teaspoon** *each* **whole allspice, mustard seed, whole black peppers, and mixed pickling spice**

In a large bowl, combine salt and water and stir until dissolved; then add onions. Cover and refrigerate for 12 to 24 hours.

Prepare 3 pint-size wide-mouth canning jars, following step 1 under "Processing with a Canning Kettle," page 49.

In a pan, stir together vinegar, brown sugar, allspice, mustard seed, black peppers, and pickling spice; bring to a boil.

Drain onions, cover with cold water, drain again, and pack in clean, hot jars. Fill jars with boiling vinegar solution to within ¼ inch from top of jar. Proceed with steps 3–10 under "Processing with a Canning Kettle," page 49. Process for 10 minutes. Makes 3 pints.

Pumpkin Pickles

Pieces of fresh pumpkin simmer gently in a spicy syrup for about an hour. Similar to pickled watermelon rind, this special preserve goes nicely with any fowl—especially turkey.

2¼ cups *each* cider vinegar and sugar
3 cups water
3 whole cinnamon sticks (*each* about 2 inches long)
15 whole cloves
1 ripe pumpkin (about 4 lbs.), stem and seeds removed

In a 5-quart pot over medium-high heat, combine vinegar, sugar, water, cinnamon, and cloves. Bring to a boil and continue boiling, uncovered, for about 10 minutes. Meanwhile, cut pumpkin into 1-inch-square pieces; you should have about 6 cups. Add pumpkin pieces and bring to a boil; reduce heat to medium and continue boiling gently for 5 minutes. Remove from heat; cover and let stand at room temperature for 1 hour. Remove cover and return to medium heat. Boil gently, turning pieces occasionally, until pieces are translucent (about 1 hour).

Meanwhile, prepare 5 half-pint canning jars, following step 1 under "Processing with a Canning Kettle," page 49. Continue with steps 3–10. Process for 10 minutes. Makes 5 half pints.

Giardiniera (Pickled Vegetables)

(Pictured on pages 42 and 47)

The brightly colored, pickled mixed vegetables you see in fancy food stores and Italian delicatessens can be made at home. They're wonderful served as appetizers or with meats.

2 or 3 packages baby carrots (*each* about ½ pound)
1 small bunch celery
2 red bell or green peppers
1 large cauliflower (about 2 lbs.)
1 pound small white boiling onions
1 cup salt
4 quarts cold water
2 quarts white vinegar
¼ cup mustard seed
2 tablespoons celery seed
1 small dried hot chili pepper
2½ cups sugar

Peel carrots; cut in half lengthwise, then into 1½-inch-long pieces; you should have 4 cups.

Remove strings from celery, cut in half lengthwise, then into 1½-inch-long pieces; you should have 3 cups. Remove and discard seeds and stems from peppers and cut into 1-inch-wide strips. Break cauliflower into 1½-inch-thick flowerets; trim stems. Peel onions. In a bowl, dissolve salt in water. Add vegetables; cover and refrigerate for 12 to 18 hours; then drain, rinse in cold water, and drain again.

Combine vinegar, mustard seed, celery seed, chili pepper, and sugar in a 6-quart stainless or enamel pan. Bring to a boil, and continue boiling for 3 minutes. Add vegetables, reduce heat, and cook, uncovered, until vegetables are almost tender (about 10 minutes). Discard chili.

Prepare 6 pint-size canning jars, following step 1 under "Processing without a Canning Kettle," page 49. Proceed with steps 3–6. Makes 6 pints.

Spicy Pickled Figs

Mild, sweet Mission figs have a most accommodating nature for pickling. The heat of the pickling process develops their sweetness and helps them absorb the spicy flavor of the vinegar bath in which they cook. The blue-black figs become a rich shade of burgundy.

The flavor is both tart and sweet, with hints of cinnamon and clove. These canned pickled figs make a good relish to accompany steaks and chops.

2½ cups sugar
1½ cups white vinegar
2 whole cinnamon sticks
1 tablespoon whole cloves
4 pounds firm, ripe Mission (or Black Mission) figs

Place sugar in a 6-quart pot; stir in vinegar, cinnamon sticks, and cloves. Over medium heat, bring mixture, uncovered, to a boil; continue boiling, stirring occasionally, until reduced to 1½ cups (about 15 minutes).

Meanwhile, gently wash figs, leaving stems intact. Add figs to vinegar solution; cover, reduce heat, and simmer figs for about 15 minutes (figs should still hold their shape). Shake pan occasionally; avoid stirring because it will break up fruit.

Prepare 4 pint-size canning jars, following step 1 under "Processing without a Canning Kettle," page 49. With a slotted spoon, lift figs from boiling syrup and pack into jars; then ladle boiling syrup into each jar, filling to within ½ inch of rim. Proceed according to steps 4–6. Makes 4 pints.

NO-FUSS PICKLING

If you have a fondness for the taste of homemade pickles but don't have the time to can, try putting up these easy-to-make pickles in an afternoon. One recipe calls for freezing, and the other two specify storing in the refrigerator.

Sweet Freezer Chips

To make sweet freezer chips, you simply layer sliced cucumbers and onions in freezer jars or containers and freeze them in a vinegar and sugar syrup. To serve, just thaw what you need.

1 medium-size mild white onion
2½ pounds (about 5 medium-size) cucumbers (unpeeled), sliced ⅛ inch thick
2 tablespoons salt
2 quarts ice cubes
4 cups sugar
2 cups cider vinegar

Thinly slice onion. Mix cucumber and onion slices with salt in large bowl; cover mixture with ice cubes and refrigerate for 2 to 3 hours.

Drain off water and discard unmelted ice cubes; do not rinse. Pack cucumber and onion slices in freezer containers or freezer jars, filling to within 1½ inches of top.

In a 2-quart pan, combine sugar and vinegar; bring to a boil, stirring, until sugar dissolves. Pour just enough hot syrup over cucumbers to cover. Place lids on containers. Cool, then freeze for at least 1 week. To thaw, place container in refrigerator for at least 8 hours. Makes about 3 pints.

Armenian Mixed Vegetables

In markets that carry Middle Eastern foods you may have discovered the jars of pickled vegetables called *tourshee*.

You can make them in a 2-gallon crock, if you like, or in 3 half-gallon jars. Layer vegetables and seasonings in the crock, then set a plate with a weight on top to keep vegetables submerged in the brine.

3 cloves garlic, peeled
1 to 3 small, dried hot chili peppers
1 pound carrots, peeled and cut into 2-inch pieces (cut large carrots in half lengthwise)
6 large stalks celery, cut into 2-inch pieces
1 medium-size cauliflower (about 1 lb.), broken into flowerets
1 head cabbage (about 2 lbs.), cut into 12 wedges
2 green or red bell peppers, seeded and cut into 1½-inch squares
2 large red onions, cut into 1-inch squares
3 teaspoons whole mixed pickling spice
3⅓ cups cider vinegar
10 cups water
5 tablespoons salt

Into a 2-gallon crock, place garlic and chili peppers; or into each of 3 half-gallon jars, drop 1 clove garlic and ⅓ to 1 chili pepper. Add carrots, celery, cauliflower, cabbage, red or green peppers, and onions to crock; or distribute vegetables equally among jars. Spoon pickling spice into crock, or spoon 1 teaspoon pickling spice into each of the jars.

In a pan over medium heat, place vinegar, water, and salt; bring to a boil and pour over vegetables. Put weight on crock or lid on jars; store in refrigerator or in a cool place (a garage or unheated room) for at least a week. Chill before serving. Makes 6 quarts.

Fresh Refrigerator Pickles

(Pictured on page 42)

Paper-thin, mildly sweet fresh pickles require no canning. Refrigerated, they stay crunchy for as long as 3 weeks.

2 large English or Armenian cucumbers (or 3 large cucumbers, *each* about 1½ inches in diameter)
1 medium-size green pepper, seeds and stems removed
1 medium-size onion, finely chopped
1 tablespoon salt
2 teaspoons celery seed
¾ cup sugar
½ cup white wine vinegar

Cut unpeeled cucumbers into 1/16-inch-thick slices. Finely chop green pepper and place in a bowl along with cucumber and onion. Sprinkle with salt and celery seed and toss gently until well blended. Let stand at room temperature for 1 hour.

Combine sugar and vinegar; stir to dissolve sugar. Pour over vegetables and toss gently until well blended. Cover and refrigerate. Pickles are ready to eat in about 24 hours. Store, covered, in refrigerator for up to 3 weeks. Makes about 5 cups.

Spiced Pickled Quinces

When ripe in September and October, the quince is most commonly used to make jelly. Yet this generally neglected fruit also makes a delicious condiment to serve with meats. It is sliced, cooked in a spiced sugar syrup, then packed in jars to be enjoyed any time. They make especially handsome Christmas gifts.

8 to 10 large quinces
  2½ cups boiling water
   16 whole cloves
    2 large oranges, cut in ¼-inch slices
    6 cups sugar
    2 cups white vinegar
    1 whole cinnamon stick

Peel, core, and cut quinces into ¾-inch wedges; you should have 12 cups. Place fruit in a large pot over medium heat; pour boiling water over fruit and cook, uncovered and stirring occasionally, until tender-crisp (about 5 minutes). Drain, reserving 1½ cups liquid. Set fruit aside.

In the same pot, combine reserved 1½ cups liquid with cloves, orange slices, sugar, vinegar, and cinnamon. Bring to a boil and boil gently, uncovered, for 10 minutes. Add quinces and boil for 30 minutes longer, stirring occasionally.

Meanwhile, prepare 6 pint-size canning jars, following step 1 under "Processing without a Canning Kettle," page 49. Proceed with steps 3–6. Makes 6 pints.

Spiced Apple Rings

Cinnamon and cloves add a spicy touch to the syrup that poaches these apple rings. For full flavor, allow the apples to stand for at least a week before using them as an accompaniment to meat. They're particularly festive during the holiday season.

    6 cups sugar
 1²/3 cups cider vinegar
    1 teaspoon red food coloring (optional)
    4 whole cinnamon sticks
    2 teaspoons whole cloves
      About 4 pounds firm, ripe Golden Delicious apples, peeled and cored

Prepare 4 pint-size canning jars, following step 1 under "Processing without a Canning Kettle," page 49.

Place sugar in a 5-quart pot along with vinegar, food coloring (if used), cinnamon, and cloves. Bring mixture to a boil, uncovered; reduce heat and simmer for 10 minutes.

Slice apples crosswise into ⅓-inch-thick rings. Add the rings to the simmering syrup and cook, turning rings occasionally, for 6 to 8 minutes or until apples are barely tender and just becoming translucent around the edges.

Proceed with steps 3–6 under "Processing without a Canning Kettle," page 49, filling jars to within ½ inch of rim. Let stand for at least 1 week before using. Makes 4 pints.

Easy Hot Dog Relish

Three basic ingredients—cucumbers, onions, and green peppers—combine with spices in this sweet-sour relish that's perfect for hot dogs and other cooked sausages.

 12 large cucumbers, peeled and cut into chunks
  4 large onions, cut into chunks
  6 green peppers, stems and seeds removed
  4 teaspoons *each* celery seed and mustard seed
  1 teaspoon salt
 ½ teaspoon ground cloves
  1 tablespoon turmeric
3½ cups cider vinegar
2½ cups sugar

Chop cucumbers, onions, and peppers in a food processor or force through a food chopper; then place in a 5 or 6-quart pot. Add celery seed, mustard seed, salt, cloves, turmeric, vinegar, and sugar. Bring mixture to a boil over high heat, stirring constantly. Reduce heat and simmer, uncovered and stirring occasionally, until mixture thickens and is reduced to about 5 pints (about 3 hours).

Meanwhile, prepare 5 pint-size canning jars, following step 1 under "Processing with a Canning Kettle," page 49. Then proceed with steps 3–10. Process for 15 minutes. Makes 5 pints.

Zucchini Relish

As any vegetable gardener knows, ripe zucchini is abundant in late summer, so tasty recipes calling for lots of zucchini are most welcome. This colorful zucchini relish has a crisp, tart flavor that makes it compatible with grilled meats.

- 5 pounds medium-size zucchini
- 6 large onions, coarsely chopped
- ½ cup salt
  Cold water
- 2 cups white wine vinegar
- 1 cup sugar
- 1 teaspoon dry mustard
- 2 teaspoons celery seed
- ½ teaspoon *each* ground cinnamon, nutmeg, and pepper
- 2 jars (about 4 oz. *each*) chopped pimentos

Place zucchini and onions in a food processor or force through a food chopper until finely chopped. Place in a bowl, sprinkle with salt, and cover with water. Cover and refrigerate for at least 4 hours or until next day.

Drain vegetables, rinse well, and then drain again. Place in a 5 or 6-quart pot along with vinegar, sugar, mustard, celery seed, cinnamon, nutmeg, pepper, and pimentos. Bring to a boil over high heat, stirring occasionally. Reduce heat and simmer, uncovered and stirring occasionally, until reduced to about 3 quarts (about 20 minutes).

Meanwhile, prepare 6 pint-size canning jars, following step 1 under "Processing with a Canning Kettle," page 49. Proceed with steps 3–10. Process for 15 minutes. Makes 6 pints.

Tomato-Apple Relish

This tomato-apple relish is sweet and particularly good spooned over grilled hamburgers and hot dogs.

- 4 pounds firm ripe tomatoes
- 3 large apples
- 4 cups finely chopped onion
- 2 *each* green and red bell peppers, seeded and finely chopped
- 1 cup *each* raisins and cider vinegar
- ¾ cup firmly packed brown sugar
- 1 tablespoon mustard seed
- 1 teaspoon *each* salt and turmeric
- 1½ teaspoons celery seed

Peel tomatoes and coarsely chop; you should have 6 cups. Peel apples and coarsely chop; you

should have 4 cups. Place tomatoes and apples in a 4 to 5-quart pot along with onion, peppers, raisins, vinegar, sugar, mustard seed, salt, turmeric, and celery seed. Bring to a boil over high heat, stirring occasionally. Reduce heat to medium-low and continue to cook, uncovered and stirring occasionally to prevent sticking, until mixture is quite thick and liquid has been absorbed, (about 1 hour).

Meanwhile, prepare 4 pint-size canning jars, following step 1 under "Processing with a Canning Kettle," page 49. Then proceed with steps 3–10. Process for 10 minutes. Makes 4 pints.

Pear & Pepper Relish

Spicy hot jalapeño peppers combine with sweet ripe pears and green and red peppers in this colorful preserve. Serve with pork, ham, or chicken entrées that would benefit from such a fiery flavor complement.

- About 2 medium-size canned jalapeño chili peppers
- 3 pounds firm, ripe pears (unpeeled), cored and chopped
- 2 *each* large green and red bell peppers, seeded and chopped (or use 3 large green peppers)
- 1 large onion, chopped
- 1½ cups *each* cider vinegar and honey
- 1 teaspoon soy sauce
- ½ teaspoon *each* ground ginger and salt

Remove and discard stem ends, any bits of blackened skin, and about half the seeds from jalapeño peppers; finely chop. You should have about 2 tablespoons jalapeño peppers. Place in a 5 or 6-quart pot and stir in pears, green and red bell peppers, onion, vinegar, honey, soy, ginger, and salt. Bring to a boil over high heat. Reduce heat and simmer, uncovered and stirring occasionally as mixture thickens, until reduced to 6 cups (about 1 hour).

Meanwhile, prepare 6 half-pint canning jars, following step 1 under "Processing with a Canning Kettle," page 49. Then proceed with steps 3–10. Process for 15 minutes. Makes 6 half pints.

FLAVORED VINEGARS

(Pictured on page 34)

Fresh garden herbs and whole spices are ideal ingredients for flavoring vinegar. Whether you grow your own herbs or buy them in a market, you'll discover that flavored vinegars are very easy to prepare and make unique gifts.

Be sure to begin the process well in advance—you'll need to let the vinegar stand for several weeks to absorb the flavors of the herbs and spices. In that time the vinegar's sharp flavor will soften and mellow, resulting in a delightful blend.

To prepare flavored vinegar, simply put herbs and spices into a decorative bottle or clean jar, fill it with cider or wine vinegar, put on the lid, and let the bottle stand in a cool, dark place without shaking. It takes 3 or 4 weeks for flavor to develop.

To speed up the process by a week or two, heat the vinegar to lukewarm (or even boiling), then pour it into a bottle over herb leaves that have been crushed or coarsely chopped. Let the bottle stand in a warm, dark place and shake it gently each day. When the flavor suits you, strain out the seasonings and discard them, then return the vinegar to the bottle.

You won't be able to use this faster method to make clear vinegar with whole herbs intact—for this you must allow more time.

Don't forget to identify the vinegar's flavor by writing it on a tag or decorative label. You may want to indicate the bottling date, too. Once you've opened vinegar, store it in a cool, dark place and use it within 3 or 4 months.

Tarragon Vinegar

Wash and dry 1 or 2 sprigs (*each* about 5 inches long) **tarragon**. Place in a pint bottle and fill with **white wine vinegar**.

Grape & Rosemary Vinegar

Wash and dry 1 leafy sprig (about 5 inches long) **rosemary** and 1 sprig **lemon thyme** (optional). Place herbs in a pint bottle with **4 whole black peppers** and 5 small fresh or canned **grapes**; fill bottle with **white wine vinegar**.

Sweet Basil & Oregano Vinegar

Wash and dry 1 leafy sprig (about 5 inches long) *each* **sweet basil** and **oregano** (or substitute 2 sprigs fresh tarragon). Place herbs in a pint bottle with **4 whole black peppers** and fill with **red wine vinegar**.

Lemon-Mint Vinegar

With a small sharp knife, cut a continuous spiral strip of peel about ¼ inch wide from 1 **lemon**. Wash and dry 2 leafy sprigs of **mint**. Place mint, lemon rind, and 6 dried **currants** in a pint bottle and fill with **white wine vinegar**.

Garlic & Green Onion Vinegar

Place 1 or 2 cloves peeled **garlic** and 1 **green onion** (about 6 inches long) in a pint bottle and fill with **white wine vinegar**.

Parsley & Black Pepper Vinegar

Wash and dry 1 leafy sprig (about 5 inches long) **parsley**. Place in a pint bottle with 8 **whole black peppers** and fill with **white wine vinegar**.

Tarragon & Garlic Vinegar

Wash and dry 1 leafy sprig (about 5 inches long) **tarragon**. Place in a pint bottle with 1 or 2 cloves of **garlic** (peeled) and fill with **red wine vinegar**.

Fresh Cranberry Relish

Deep red cranberry relish shows off handsomely in jars and makes a tasty condiment to serve with the traditional holiday bird or other meats.

- 1 **pound (about 4 cups) cranberries, rinsed**
- 1 **medium-size orange**
- 1 **cup *each* raisins and cider vinegar**
- 1 **medium-size onion, chopped**
- ½ **cup chopped green pepper**
- 1 **clove garlic, minced or pressed**
- 2 **tablespoons minced fresh ginger**
- 1 **can (6 oz.) frozen cranberry juice concentrate, thawed**
- 2 **cups sugar**
- ½ **teaspoon salt**
- 1 **teaspoon mustard seed**
- ¼ **teaspoon *each* cayenne and ground cloves**

Coarsely chop cranberries and place in a 4 or 5-quart pot. With a vegetable peeler, remove zest (colored part of peel) from orange. Cut zest into thin julienne strips and add to pot. Holding orange over pot to catch juice, peel off and discard white membrane. Separate orange sections and stir into pot. Add raisins, vinegar, onion, green pepper, garlic, ginger, and cranberry juice.

Bring mixture to a boil over high heat, stirring occasionally; boil, uncovered and stirring occasionally, for 10 minutes. Stir in sugar, salt, mustard seed, cayenne, and cloves. Reduce heat and boil gently, stirring often, until mixture thickens (about 20 minutes).

Meanwhile, prepare 5 half-pint canning jars, following step 1 under "Processing with a Canning Kettle," page 49. Then proceed with steps 3–10. Process for 10 minutes. Makes 5 half pints.

Whole Cranberry Orange Sauce

Tart, whole-berry cranberry sauce, a traditional holiday relish, is easy to put up in jars. In this recipe, the berries are accented with orange juice and sweetened with brown sugar.

- 1 **pound (about 4 cups) cranberries, rinsed**
- 2 **cups firmly packed brown sugar**
- 3 **tablespoons frozen orange juice concentrate, thawed**
- 1¼ **cups water**

Combine berries, sugar, orange juice concentrate, and water in a 3 or 4-quart pot. Bring mixture to a boil over high heat, stirring occasionally. Continue to boil, uncovered and stirring occasionally, until most of the berries open (about 5 minutes).

Meanwhile, prepare 4 half-pint canning jars, following step 1 under "Processing with a Canning Kettle," page 49. Then proceed with steps 3–10. Process for 15 minutes. Makes 4 half pints.

Apricot Chutney

This light-colored apricot chutney is medium hot. For a milder version, omit the seeds from the peppers or use fewer peppers than the recipe specifies.

- 1 **cup *each* granulated sugar, firmly packed brown sugar, currants, and cider vinegar**
- 1 **tablespoon finely chopped fresh ginger (or ¾ teaspoon ground ginger)**
- 1 **teaspoon *each* dry mustard and ground allspice**
  Dash ground cloves
- 3 **small dried hot chili peppers, crushed**
- 2 **tablespoons tamarind syrup (optional)**
- 1 **small lime, seeded and chopped**
- ½ **cup chopped onion**
- 1 **small clove garlic, minced or pressed**
- 4 **pounds apricots, pitted and quartered**

Combine granulated sugar, brown sugar, currants, vinegar, ginger, mustard, allspice, cloves, peppers, tamarind syrup (if you wish), lime, onion, and garlic in a 4 to 5-quart pot. Bring mixture to a boil, stir in apricots, and return to a boil. Reduce heat and simmer, uncovered and stirring often to prevent sticking, until slightly thickened (about 45 minutes).

Prepare 4 pint-size canning jars, following step 1 under "Processing with a Canning Kettle," page 49. Then proceed with steps 3–10. Process for 5 minutes. Makes 4 pints.

Tomato-Pear Chutney

Late summer often brings you more tomatoes than you can use at one time. Why not preserve some of your harvest as chutney?

2 pounds tomatoes, peeled

2 pounds firm, ripe pears, peeled and cored

2 large green peppers, seeded and chopped

2 cups firmly packed brown sugar

1 cup white vinegar

2 teaspoons salt

1 teaspoon *each* ground ginger and dry mustard

¼ teaspoon cayenne

¾ cup coarsely chopped candied ginger

2 cans (about 8 oz. *each*) water chestnuts, drained and sliced

1 jar (4 oz.) diced pimentos

Dice tomatoes and pears; you should have 8 cups total. Place pears in a 5-quart pot along with peppers, sugar, vinegar, salt, ginger, mustard, and cayenne. Bring to a boil over high heat. Stir in tomatoes, reduce heat to medium and boil gently, uncovered and stirring often, until mixture thickens slightly (about 1 hour).

Stir in candied ginger, water chestnuts, and pimentos. Boil gently, uncovered and stirring often until thickened (10 to 15 minutes).

Meanwhile, prepare 4 pint-size canning jars, following step 1 under "Processing with a Canning Kettle," page 49. Proceed with steps 3–10. Process for 5 minutes. Makes 4 pints.

Papaya-Plum Chutney

(Pictured on page 34)

Colorful papayas and firm, red plums make an unusual taste combination in this easy-to-make chutney.

1¼ cups cider vinegar

1¾ cups sugar

½ cup golden raisins

2 cloves garlic, minced or pressed

3 tablespoons chopped crystallized ginger

1 whole cinnamon stick

1½ teaspoons salt

⅛ to ¼ teaspoon cayenne

2 large (about 1 lb. *each*) ripe papayas

2 pounds firm red plums

Combine vinegar, sugar, raisins, garlic, ginger, cinnamon, salt, and cayenne in a heavy 4 or 5-quart pot. Bring to a boil over high heat. Reduce heat and simmer, uncovered and stirring often, until thickened (about 1½ hours).

Peel papayas, cut in half, and discard seeds. Cut fruit into ½-inch squares. Quarter plums, discarding pits. Add fruit to vinegar mixture and continue simmering, uncovered and stirring occasionally, until papaya is tender (about 30 minutes). Discard cinnamon stick.

Meanwhile, prepare 3 pint-size canning jars, following step 1 under "Processing with a Canning Kettle," page 49. Proceed with steps 3–10. Process for 5 minutes. Makes 3 pints.

Mango-Peach Chutney

Mangoes make delicious, traditional-style chutneys. Unfortunately though, they can be quite costly. One way to stretch their flavor is to combine them with peaches.

1½ cups *each* sugar and white vinegar

1 large onion, chopped

1 green pepper, seeded and diced

1 clove garlic, minced or pressed

1 lime, seeded and thinly sliced

1½ teaspoons ground cinnamon

½ teaspoon *each* ground cloves and allspice

1 teaspoon salt

⅛ to ¼ teaspoon cayenne

½ cup raisins

3 large (about 2½ lbs. *total*) ripe mangoes

2 pounds peaches

Combine sugar, vinegar, onion, pepper, garlic, lime, cinnamon, cloves, allspice, salt, cayenne, and raisins in a heavy 4 to 5-quart pot. Bring mixture to a boil, reduce heat and simmer, uncovered and stirring often to prevent sticking, until thickened (about 1 hour).

Peel, pit, and slice mangoes; you should have about 3½ cups fruit. Peel and slice peaches. Add mangoes and peaches to syrup and simmer, uncovered and stirring occasionally, until fruit is tender (about 30 minutes).

Meanwhile, prepare 3 pint-size canning jars, following step 1 under "Processing with a Canning Kettle," page 49. Then proceed with steps 3–10. Process for 5 minutes. Makes 3 pints.

LABELS, TAGS & TRIMS

Whether your canned goods fill your own shelves or make their way to friends as gifts, you can decorate—and identify—the jars with your own personalized labels, tags, and trims. Make them as simple or elaborate as you like; the materials are everywhere, from your own stationery supplies to packaged tags made especially for canning jars.

For labels and tags, take advantage of the return of the old-fashioned rubber stamp and ink pad. You can buy a set of letters and spell out the contents, or purchase individual decorative stamps, such as a strawberry, a duck, or an abstract design. Pointing hands or stamps that read "Do not open till . . ." add humor to your labels and tags. Experiment on scratch paper until you get the look you want.

A label attached to a jar should allow enough space to write the contents and date. You'll find special jar labels printed with "Contents" and "From the kitchen of" at stationery and some office supply stores.

To make your own labels, consider these ideas:

• Office supply stores are full of plain labels, decals, and stickers that make simple, inexpensive jar labels. Among them are plain gummed mailing labels, narrow adhesive file folder labels, and blank name tags or badges. Some stores also carry unusual adhesive labels with old-fashioned drawings.

• "Visiting cards," those small white cards from another era, offer unlimited possibilities for labels. Attach cards with decorative tape, gummed stickers, or the new adhesive stickers that come in a variety of playful shapes from teddy bears to rainbows. Plain place cards, small notepaper, and gift enclosure cards also work as labels.

Tie on tags when your canned goods are for gifts. We present a few suggestions; you're sure to come up with more just from browsing through your gift wrap and stationery supplies.

• The visiting cards mentioned above become beautiful tags when you cover one side with wrapping paper or adhesive-backed fabric (available at some fabric stores); round adhesive seals with an initial give a personal touch. Punch a hole in one corner of the card, thread with ribbon, yarn, cord, or string, and tie around the neck of the jar—or, on an old-fashioned jar, tie to the clamp.

• Plain baggage tags are inexpensive and are available in a variety of sizes. Replace the string with festive ribbon or yarn and decorate with stamps or stickers. In some stores you'll also find plain tags in bright colors.

• Recipe cards become ideal tags when you want to give instructions along with the food. Simply punch a hole in one corner and attach with ribbon or yarn. For a tag that can go right into a recipe file, tie the card (with-

out punching a hole) around the middle of the jar with a pretty ribbon. You can even make your own ribbon by cutting strips of fabric with pinking shears.

• If you receive seed catalogs or collect pretty pictures of fruits and vegetables, cut out photos and glue them to cards or paper. For matching tags, use a berry for blackberry jam, a tomato for canned tomatoes, a cucumber for a jar of pickles.

Fancy trims take labels and tags one step further for extra special gifts:

• Decorate the sides of jars with adhesive stickers—hearts or circles or whatever strikes your imagination.

• Remember the continuous fabric name tags you can order printed with a name? Cut apart, they're usually stitched into clothing. If you're putting up lots of plum jam, for example, why not order them printed with "Chris's Plum Jam." Tie a length around each jar and make a bow for a subtle and unusual trim.

• Fold a paper doily over the top of a jar, encircle with ribbon, yarn, or cord tied in a bow, and decorate with a sprig of baby's breath, artificial flowers or berries, or tiny pine cones.

• If you're giving dehydrated food in a plain canning jar, cover the lid with adhesive-backed fabric—the jar becomes a charming container to use again and again.

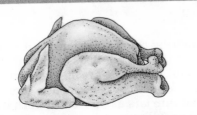

CANNING MEAT, POULTRY & SEAFOOD

If you've raised chickens for the county fair or have purchased a side of beef for the winter, you may be facing storage problems. Freezing is the easiest method of keeping meats, poultry, and fish fresh; it also offers the greatest versatility (see page 96). However, if you don't have a freezer, or if you live in an area that's subject to power failures, consider canning the meat. (Meats purchased frozen also may be defrosted and canned at home.)

Meats that can well are beef, veal, lamb, pork, chicken, turkey, rabbit, game birds, and small and large game animals. On page 65, techniques are given for canning fish.

The first thing to know about canning meats is that it can be done—simply, safely, and with results that are nutritious and tasty. But there are dangers involved—you *must* use the right equipment and you *must* follow directions to the letter; anything less spells failure, and where home canning of low-acid foods (vegetables, meat, poultry, and fish) is concerned, failure can be fatal.

The only safe way to can meat, poultry, or fish is in a steam pressure canner under specific amounts of pressure, holding a temperature of 240°F for specific periods, as shown in the chart on page 69. At high elevations, pressure adjustments are necessary; these are indicated in a note at the top of the chart. As a safety precaution, even the most carefully canned meats and seafood should be heated to a boil and then simmered hard (205° to 210°F) for 15 minutes before they're served.

Here are some ways *not* to can meats, poultry, or fish—they are all fraught with danger: Never process meat in a regular canning kettle, using the water bath method prescribed for canning fruits and tomatoes—the heat of this method is not sufficient to prevent dangerous spoilage in low-acid foods. Nor can the everyday "pressure cooker"—the one designed for fast cooking—be used for canning. Don't try to use a steam pressure canner without pressure, and finally, never use the old-fashioned oven canning method; an oven provides too slow a rate of heat transfer, as well as uneven heat distribution. Any of the preceding methods leaves you open to the dangerous—potentially fatal—risk of botulism (for more information on botulism, see page 37).

If you slaughter your own animals, chill the meat immediately afterwards to prevent spoilage and permit tenderizing. The meat is much easier to handle when it is cold. Keep meat at a temperature below 40°F until time to can it. Can it within a few days of slaughter.

If refrigeration is not available and the maximum daily temperature is above 40°F, process the meat as soon as the animal's body heat is gone.

If the meat must be held for more than a few days, freeze and store it at 0°F or below. Before canning, cut or saw the frozen meat into pieces of desired size and thaw it in the refrigerator at 40°F or lower until the ice crystals have gone.

Of course, you should always keep meat clean. Rinse poultry thoroughly in cold water and drain before canning.

If you catch your own fish, can or freeze it as soon as possible. Clean immediately and chill it after the catch; keep it chilled until you're ready to preserve it. If no refrigeration is handy, rub it with salt or cover it with a wet cloth.

Equipment you'll need

Canning equipment for meat or fish is the same as for vegetables—carefully read the information under "Equipment you'll need," page 36. The steam pressure canner is the essential piece of equipment. An accurate meat thermometer is also necessary for measuring the temperature in the packed, unsealed jars of food.

Two ways to pack meat & poultry into jars

Before you can begin processing meat or poultry, it must be properly packed into canning jars, using one of the methods described on page 64. Additional details—adapting the following methods to specific meats as necessary—are included in the chart on page 69; be sure to read the chart carefully before proceeding.

The hot-pack method involves precooking the meat or poultry before it is packed into canning jars. The hot meat—usually cooked until medium done—is packed into hot jars; then boiling broth or water is poured over the meat in the jars. Salt may be added, but it's for flavor—it doesn't act as a preservative. The temperature of the meat in the jars at the time they are sealed should be 170°F (checked periodically with the meat thermometer).

The raw-pack method involves packing uncooked meat into unheated canning jars. The open jars are then placed on a rack in a large pan of boiling water (such as the pressure canner, used without the pressure gauge). The jars should be spaced so they don't touch the canner sides or each other; the water should rise to within 2 inches of the open jar tops, but no higher. The canner is then covered and the jars simmered until the temperature in the center of the food inside the jars is 170°F (check periodically with the meat thermometer). The cooking process exhausts the air from the jars and creates a vacuum in the jars after sealing and processing. It also helps prevent changes in flavor.

Step-by-step canning for meat & poultry

1 Carefully read all the preceding information on canning meats, and check the meat chart on page 69 for instructions for the particular meat or poultry you're about to can. (To can fish, read the step-by-step instructions on page 65.) Also read the section on "Equipment you'll need," page 63.

2 Get out steam pressure canner, jars (discard any that have nicks or cracks), ring bands, lids (they must be new), and other items you need. Be sure all equipment is clean and ready to use. Discard any bent or rusted ring bands. Scald lids in boiling water; keep in very hot water until time to use. Place jars in a kettle of very hot water.

3 Place pressure canner on range element, put rack into canner, and pour in hot water to a depth of 2 or 3 inches (enough to keep canner from boiling dry; when jars are put in, water should rise no higher than to within 2 inches of jar tops). Cover canner loosely and turn on range element to medium-high to bring

water to a boil; keep it hot while you prepare meat.

4 Following chart directions, and referring to one of the two methods for packing meat into jars (at left), prepare only enough meat for one canner load at a time. Pack meat into jars as instructed in chart, filling jars as full as possible.

Stand filled jars in very hot water (a regular canning kettle works nicely) and fill remaining jars one at a time. Add boiling broth or water as necessary, following chart instructions; be sure to leave correct head space. Run a narrow spatula around each jar between food and jar sides, to release any air bubbles; add more liquid if necessary.

To exhaust air from jars, heat contents to 170°F

5 Wipe jar rim with damp cloth to remove any food particles or fat that might prevent a seal. Lift a jar lid from hot water and place it on jar (if lids stick together, plunge into cold water, then hot). Screw ring band on by hand; do not overtighten. Repeat with remaining jars.

6 Turn heat to medium-high. Place jars on rack in canner, spaced so they don't touch canner sides or each other. If using two layers of jars, stagger top layer on a rack placed between the layers, so that steam can circulate freely.

7 Before processing, you must vent pressure canner to eliminate all air inside. To do this, fasten down canner lid, leaving petcock open (or vent pipe uncovered) and let a jet of steam escape for at least 10 minutes. (Air left in canner would prevent temperature from rising as high as necessary for canning, resulting in uneven heat distribution and possible spoilage.)

8 After venting canner, close petcock (or put on weighted gauge) and bring canner to 10 pounds pressure (240°F). Then immediately start counting the processing time, as indicated on chart, making sure pressure gauge never falls below required level—you'll have to watch gauge constantly and regulate heating element as necessary. Do not lower pressure by opening petcock. Keep drafts from reaching the canner. Watch timing and pressure carefully—fluctuating pressure during processing causes liquid to be drawn out of jars.

9 After processing, remove canner from heat to another range element—never to a cold surface. Canner will be heavy; be careful not to tilt it—toppled jars may not seal.

10 Let canner cool gradually—it will take about ½ hour; never try to speed the process under cold water. About 2 minutes after pressure has returned to zero on gauge, slowly open petcock (or remove weighted gauge).

11 Allow canner to cool for about 15 minutes after opening petcock. Then remove lid by opening canner away from you so you don't get steam in your face. Leave jars in canner 10 to 15 minutes longer—*do not disturb seal.*

12 At end of cooling time, remove jars with a jar lifter (see illustration on page 41). Set jars on a folded cloth or board—never on a cold surface. Leave enough room between jars for air to circulate. You'll notice bubbling going on in jars—this indicates they are properly sealed, and contents are still boiling under vacuum. When jars are cool, remove ring bands, if desired. (To loosen a band that sticks, cover with a hot, damp cloth for 1 to 2 minutes; then loosen.)

13 Test seal by pressing lid with your finger. If it stays down when pressed, jar is sealed (see illustration on page 9); if lid pops back up, it is not sealed.

If a jar hasn't sealed by the time it's cool, refrigerate and use meat or poultry within a few days—if it looks and smells all right. Or if you want to recan it, be aware that much of the food value and flavor will be lost, since you must process the jar again for the full length of time. It will be safe to eat, though, if it seals on the second try. Use a new lid—a lid that's been through the processing stage won't seal.

14 If, for some reason, you didn't follow directions in every detail, be aware of food poisoning by reading the information about botulism on page 37 and follow directions.

15 Label and store jars in a cool, dark place.

16 For ultimate safety, some authorities recommend the following procedure for any home-canned, low-acid foods: before serving, bring to a boil and then hard simmer (205° to 210°F) for 15 minutes.

Step-by-step canning for fish

1 Carefully read the preceding information under "Canning Meat, Poultry & Seafood" on page 63 and "Equipment you'll need" on the same page.

2 Thoroughly scale fish with a fish-scaling knife or other knife with a dull blade, scraping from tail to head. Remove fins, cut off head and tail, and wash body cavities thoroughly.

3 Split fish lengthwise along backbone. Remove backbone, leaving as little flesh as possible on bone. Cut large fish into jar-length pieces, 2 inches wide.

4 Prepare a brine by combining ¾ cup salt with 1 gallon water (this amount is sufficient for 25 pounds of fish). Place pieces of fish in brine to soak for 1 hour.

5 Get out steam pressure canner, pint-size jars (quart-size jars are not recommended because processing time would be too long; discard any jars that have nicks or cracks), ring bands, lids (they must be new), and other items you need. Be sure all equipment is clean and ready to use. Discard any bent or rusted ring bands. Scald lids in boiling water; keep in very hot water until time to use. Place jars in a kettle of very hot water.

6 Place pressure canner on range element, put rack into canner, and pour in hot water to a depth of 2 to 3 inches (enough to keep canner from boiling dry; when jars are put in, water should rise no higher than to within 2 inches of jar tops). Cover canner loosely and turn on

(Continued on next page)

range element to medium-high to bring water to a boil; keep it hot while you finish preparing fish.

7 After soaking for 1 hour, drain fish well for 10 minutes. Pack jars as full as possible with fish, arranging pieces with skin side next to glass (alternate head and tail ends if small whole fish are used). Do not add more brine or water.

8 Wipe jar rim with a damp cloth to remove any food particles that might prevent a seal. Lift a jar lid from hot water and place it on jar (if lids stick together, plunge into cold water, then hot). Screw ring band on by hand; don't overtighten. Repeat with remaining jars.

9 Turn heat to medium-high. Place jars on rack in canner, spaced so they don't touch canner sides or each other. If using two layers of jars, stagger top layer on a rack placed between the layers, so that steam can circulate freely.

10 Before processing, you must vent pressure canner to eliminate all air inside. To do this, fasten down canner lid, leaving petcock open (or vent pipe uncovered) and let a jet of steam escape for 10 minutes. (Air left in canner would prevent temperature from rising as high as necessary for canning, resulting in uneven heat distribution and possible spoilage.)

11 After venting canner, close petcock (or put on weighted gauge) and bring canner to 10 pounds pressure (240°F). Then immediately start counting the processing time of 1 hour and 50 minutes, making sure pressure gauge never falls below required level—you'll have to watch gauge constantly and regulate heating element as necessary. Do not lower pressure by opening petcock. Keep drafts from reaching canner. Watch timing and pressure carefully—fluctuating pressure during processing causes liquid to be drawn out of jars.

12 After processing, remove canner from heat to another range element—never to a cold surface. Canner will be heavy; be careful not to tilt it—toppled jars may not seal.

13 Let canner cool gradually—it will take about ½ hour; never try to speed the process under cold water. About 2 minutes after pressure

has returned to zero on gauge, slowly open petcock (or remove weighted gauge).

14 Allow canner to cool for about 15 minutes after opening petcock. Then remove lid by opening canner away from you so you don't get steam in your face. Leave jars in canner 10 to 15 minutes longer—*do not disturb seal*.

15 At end of cooling time, remove jars with a jar lifter. Set on a folded cloth or board—never on a cold surface. Leave enough room between jars for air to circulate. You'll notice bubbling going on in jars—this indicates they are properly sealed and contents are still boiling under vacuum. When jars are cool, remove ring bands, if desired. (To loosen a band that sticks, cover with a hot, damp cloth for 1 to 2 minutes; then loosen.)

16 Test seal by pressing lid with your finger. If it stays down when pressed, jar is sealed (see illustration on page 9). If lid pops back up, it is not sealed.
   If a jar hasn't sealed by the time it's cool, refrigerate and use fish within a few days—if it cooks and smells all right. Or if you want to recan it, be aware that much of the food value and flavor will be lost, since you must process the jar again for the full length of time. It will be safe to eat, though, if it seals on the second try. Use a new lid—a lid that's been through the processing stage won't seal.

17 If, for some reason, you didn't follow directions in every detail, be aware of food poisoning by reading "Guard Against Botulism," page 37.

18 Store jars in a cool, dark place.

19 For ultimate safety, some authorities recommend the following procedure for any home-canned, low-acid foods: before serving, bring to a boil and then hard simmer (205° to 210°F) for 15 minutes.

Meat Recipes

Chili Con Carne

Spiced with chili powder, oregano, and ground cumin, this meaty chili dish goes well with homemade cornbread or muffins.

  1 **pound dry pink or red beans**
  4 **pounds beef stew meat, cut in ½-inch cubes**
  3 **tablespoons salad oil**
  1 **large onion, sliced**
  1 **clove garlic, minced or pressed**
  1 **quart canned tomatoes (see chart on page 11) or peeled, chopped fresh tomatoes**
  2½ **teaspoons salt**
  2 **teaspoons *each* chili powder and oregano leaves**
  ½ **teaspoon ground cumin**

Soak beans overnight in enough water to cover. (Or cover them with water and bring to a boil, simmer for 2 minutes, remove from heat, and let soak for 1 hour.) Drain beans well (reserving liquid); set aside.

In a wide frying pan over medium heat, brown beef in oil. Place in a 4 or 5-quart pot along with beans, onion, garlic, tomatoes, salt, chili powder, oregano, cumin, and about 3 cups of the reserved liquid. Bring to a boil; reduce heat and simmer, covered and stirring occasionally, for about 1½ hours (adding more liquid as needed to keep beans from sticking to pot).

Prepare and fill 3 quart-size canning jars, following steps 1–16 on page 64 and using the hot-pack method (do not add boiling water or broth). Process for 1 hour and 30 minutes. Makes 3 quarts.

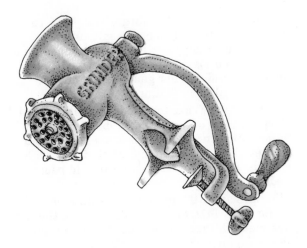

Traditional Mincemeat

(Pictured on page 34)

For holiday baking, many modern cooks purchase their mincemeat in jars or packages. But if you read the labels, you'll discover commercial mincemeat contains mostly fruit and sweeteners with little or no meat.

This old-fashioned mincemeat recipe begins the traditional way—with meat. However, instead of the more expensive beef with additional suet, this calls for pork butt.

  1 **tablespoon salad oil**
  2 **pounds boneless pork butt, untrimmed and cut into ½-inch cubes**
  1 **quart apple juice**
  2 **quarts peeled and cubed apples (about 6 large)**
  2 **medium-size oranges, rinsed, seeded and chopped**
  3 **tablespoons lemon juice**
  1 **pound dark brown sugar**
  1½ **teaspoons *each* salt, ground nutmeg, ginger, and cloves**
  1 **tablespoon ground cinnamon**
  1 **package (about 12 oz.) pitted prunes, halved**
  1 **package (8 oz.) pitted dates, halved**
  1 **package (12 oz.) golden raisins**
  ¾ **cup brandy or substitute ½ cup apple juice mixed with ½ teaspoon brandy flavoring**

Heat oil in a heavy 6 to 8-quart pot over medium heat. Cook half of the pork cubes until lightly browned. Remove from pot with slotted spoon and set aside; cook remaining pork. Return all pork cubes to pan; stir in apple juice, apples, oranges, lemon juice, sugar, salt, nutmeg, ginger, cloves, and cinnamon. Bring mixture to a boil over medium heat. Boil gently, uncovered and stirring often, for about 45 minutes.

Stir in prunes, dates, and raisins. Continue cooking, uncovered, for 15 minutes or until mincemeat is thick but still juicy. Remove from heat and stir in brandy.

Prepare and fill 4 quart-size canning jars, following steps 1–16 on page 64 and using the hot-pack method (don't add boiling water or broth). Process for 30 minutes. Makes 4 quarts.

Tomato Meat Sauce

Here's a meaty tomato sauce loaded with vegetables and herbs. Serve it, heated, over any type of pasta—rigatoni, gnocchi, or spaghetti; top with grated Parmesan or Romano cheese.

(Continued on next page)

2 tablespoons salad oil
About 12 ounces mild Italian
  sausages
2 medium-size onions, chopped
½ pound lean ground beef
2 cloves garlic, minced or pressed
2 carrots, peeled and finely chopped
2 stalks celery, chopped
½ pound mushrooms, sliced
2 cans (6 oz. *each*) tomato paste
2 quarts canned tomatoes (see chart
  on page 11) or peeled, chopped fresh
  tomatoes
1 cup dry red wine
2 teaspoons basil
¼ teaspoon sage
1 cup chopped parsley
1 teaspoon salt
½ teaspoon pepper

Heat oil in a 3 or 4-quart pot over medium heat. Remove casings from sausages, crumble, and brown in oil. Stir in onions and cook until tender. Add ground beef and cook until well browned. Stir in garlic, carrot, celery, and mushrooms; cook for 1 or 2 minutes, then stir in tomato paste, tomatoes and their liquid (breaking up tomatoes with a spoon), wine, basil, sage, parsley, salt, and pepper.

Bring to a boil; reduce heat and simmer, covered and stirring occasionally, for 1½ to 2 hours or until sauce is thickened and flavors are well blended. Skim off and discard fat.

Prepare and fill 5 pint-size canning jars, following steps 1–16 on page 64 and using hot-pack method (do not add boiling water or broth). Process for 1 hour and 5 minutes. Makes 5 pints.

Simmered Corned Beef

You cook this corned beef in a flavorful liquid, then let it chill overnight in the cooking liquid before canning.

About 5 pounds corned beef, bottom
  round or brisket
Water
1 medium-size onion, chopped
¼ teaspoon *each* garlic powder and
  liquid hot pepper seasoning
1 teaspoon dill weed
3 bay leaves
2 whole cinnamon sticks
5 whole cloves
1 orange, rinsed and thinly sliced

Put corned beef in a Dutch oven; add 2 quarts water. Cover, bring to a boil, reduce heat, and simmer for 30 minutes. Taste water; if salty, drain water from beef and discard it. Add 2 quarts fresh water to beef.

Stir in onion, garlic powder, liquid hot pepper seasoning, dill, bay, cinnamon, cloves, and orange slices. Cover, bring water to a boil, reduce heat, and simmer for 2½ to 3 hours or until meat is tender when pierced. Cool, cover, and chill overnight.

Remove meat from broth (save broth for other uses) and slice meat or cut into 1-inch chunks.

Prepare and fill 4 pint-size canning jars, following steps 1–16 on page 64 and using the hot-pack method (do not add boiling water or broth). Process for 1 hour and 15 minutes. Makes 4 pints.

Beef & Vegetable Soup

You might offer sour cream at the table to add to individual servings of this whole-meal soup. Do not substitute your own soup recipe; the processing time may differ.

3 pounds boneless lean beef, cut in
  1-inch cubes
6 cups water
About 2 teaspoons salt
About ½ teaspoon pepper
2 cloves garlic, minced or pressed
1 whole bay leaf
⅓ cup pearl barley or rice
1 quart canned tomatoes (see chart on
  page 11) or peeled, chopped fresh
  tomatoes
4 stalks celery, sliced
4 large carrots, sliced
2 medium-size onions, cut in wedges
½ small head cabbage, coarsely
  shredded
2 cans (about 1 lb. *each*) red kidney
  beans

In a Dutch oven or other large, heavy pot, combine meat, water, 2 teaspoons salt, and ½ teaspoon pepper. Bring slowly to a boil, spooning off any foam that rises to the top. Add garlic and bay. Cover and simmer gently for about 1¼ hours or until meat is tender.

Add barley or rice, tomatoes (including liquid), celery, carrots, onions, and cabbage. Cover and simmer until the vegetables are tender (about 20 minutes). Add beans, including their liquid; heat through. Taste, and add more salt and pepper, if needed.

Prepare and fill 7 quart-size canning jars, following steps 1–16 on page 64 and using the hot-pack method. Process for 1 hour and 55 minutes. Makes 7 quarts.

Guide for Canning Meat & Poultry

NOTE: At elevations higher than 1,000 feet, increase pressure of steam pressure canner, adding 1 pound for elevations between 1,001 and 2,000 feet, and 1 pound for each additional 1,000 feet. Processing times remain the same.

Food	How to prepare	Processing time at 10 pounds pressure Pints	Quarts
Meat, cut-up	Cut meat from bone, trimming away most fat without unduly slashing lean part of meat. Cut tender meat into strips about 1" shorter than jars, so grain runs lengthwise. Cut less tender pieces in chunks as for stew.		
	Hot pack: Put meat in large shallow pan; add just enough water to keep it from sticking. Cover; precook slowly until medium done (so almost no red color shows when chunks are cut in center). Stir occasionally for even heat distribution. Pack hot meat loosely into jars, leaving 1" space at top. Add salt, if desired (½ teaspoon to pints, 1 teaspoon to quarts). Cover meat with boiling meat broth.* Apply lid and ring band.	75 min.	90 min.
	Raw pack: Pack raw meat loosely into jars, leaving 1" space at top. Place open jars in kettle of boiling water and heat slowly until temperature in center of food inside jars is 170° (see page 64). If you don't have a thermometer, heat for 75 minutes. Add salt as for hot pack. Apply lid and ring band.	·75 min.	90 min.
Meat, ground	Grind small pieces of fresh, lean meat, never mixing leftover scraps or lumps of fat with fresh meat. Add 1 teaspoon salt for each pound of ground meat, mixing well. Shape ground meat into fairly thin patties that can be packed into jars without breaking. Precook patties in a 325° oven until medium done (so almost no red color shows when cut in center). Skim off and discard all fat. Pack patties into jars, leaving 1" space at top. Cover with boiling meat broth,* leaving 1" head space. Apply lid and ring band.	75 min.	90 min.
Sausage	Use your favorite sausage recipe but go lightly on seasoning as they change flavor in canning and storage. (Omit sage; it makes canned sausage bitter.) Shape into patties, precook, pack, and process as directed for ground meat, above.	75 min.	90 min.
Poultry, cut-up	Debone breast; cut drumsticks off short; leave bone in other meaty pieces. Trim off fat. Use bony pieces for making broth or stock.		
	Hot pack with bone: Place raw poultry in a pan and cover with hot broth* or water. Put on lid; heat, stirring occasionally, until medium done. To test, cut piece at center; if pink is almost gone, meat is ready. Pack loosely in jars. Place thighs and drumsticks with skin next to glass. Fit breast and small pieces into center. Leave 1" space at top. Add salt if desired (½ teaspoon for pints, 1 teaspoon for quarts). Cover with boiling cooking broth*, leaving 1" head space. Apply lid and ring band.	65 min.	75 min.
	Hot pack without bone: Remove all bones from poultry (leaving skin) either before or after precooking as above. Pack jars loosely with hot poultry, following directions given above, leaving 1" space above poultry. Add salt if desired (½ teaspoon for pints, 1 teaspoon for quarts). Pour in boiling broth* leaving 1" head space. Apply lid and ring band.	75 min.	90 min.
	Raw pack with bone: Pack raw poultry loosely in jar, placing thighs and drumsticks with skin next to glass. Fit breast and small pieces into center. Leave 1" space at top. Simmer poultry in jars until food in center of jar reaches 170° (see page 64). If you don't have a thermometer, simmer until medium done (about 75 minutes). Add salt if desired (½ teaspoon for pints or 1 teaspoon for quarts). Apply lid and ring band.	65 min.	75 min.
Stock, Beef or Chicken	**Hot Pack:** Make stock fairly concentrated. Cover bony pieces of meat or chicken with lightly salted water. Simmer until tender. Skim off fat and remove bones, leaving meat in stock. Pour boiling soup stock into jars, leaving 1" head space. Apply lid and ring band.	20 min.	25 min.

*** TO MAKE MEAT OR POULTRY BROTH, place bony pieces in a pan and cover with cold water. Bring to a boil; reduce heat and simmer until meat is tender. Pour broth into another pan; skim off fat. Add boiling broth to canning jars packed with precooked meat or poultry; fill to level specified in directions.**

About canning . . .

Q Is it safe to can food in empty mayonnaise jars or other similar jars?

A If the jars can be fitted with canning lids and screw-type ring bands AND if you're canning fruit, jam, or other preserves that can safely be canned by the water bath method, it is now considered safe to use jars other than those sold just for canning. However, you must check these jars for nicks and cracks as directed in step 1 on page 8. Never use ordinary jars when processing in a steam pressure canner—they are less tolerant to heat shock.

Q What foods are safe to can by the water bath method?

A All fruits, fruit juices, fruit purées, tomatoes, and pickles.

Q What foods require the steam pressure method?

A All vegetables (except tomatoes and pickles), meat, poultry, and fish.

Q Is it normal for lids to make a popping sound after jars are removed from the canning kettle?

A Yes. It means the sealing process has been completed.

Q Is it all right to reuse canning lids?

A No. The sealing compound is damaged by first use; lids won't seal again. Ring bands can be used repeatedly, though, if they're in good shape.

Q Can foods be processed in the oven?

A No. Jars may explode; also, the temperature of the food in the jars during processing would be variable and could lead to spoilage.

Q If ring bands come loose during canning, should they be tightened afterwards?

A No. Tighten sufficiently before canning. Their purpose is to keep the lids in place and to help seal the jars. Retightening may break the seal. In any case, they're often removed after the food cools.

Q What makes the undersides of metal lids turn dark?

A The natural components such as acids and salts in some foods may corrode the metal and cause harmless brown or black deposits to form under the lid. They won't hurt you.

Q Is it all right to let the jars cool in the water in which they were processed?

A No. The food will keep right on cooking in the water, giving you overcooked food.

Q Is it all right to double a favorite jam recipe?

A No. Doubling the quantities is asking for trouble because rapidly heating large amounts from the bottom only is difficult.

Q What if the jar seals and then later comes open?

A This is caused by the production of gas from microbes still alive in the food. It may be a sign of growth of botulism bacteria in low-acid foods.

About fruit . . .

Q Do fruits have to be canned with white sugar?

A No. Fruit juice, water, or honey may be used instead.

Q Why should ascorbic acid be added to fruit?

A Ascorbic acid (vitamin C), an antidarkening agent, retards oxidation that browns foods. It keeps foods looking attractive and retards the loss of vitamins.

Q What causes fruit to float?

A Fruit syrup may have been too heavy; or fruit may have been overripe; or fruit may not have been packed tightly enough into the jar. Some fruits such as apricots and plums contain enough gas to cause floating.

Q Why does fruit sometimes darken at the top of the jar?

A Prepared cut fruit may have been exposed to the air too long; or liquid in the jar may not have covered the food; or too much head space may have been left in the jar; or air bubbles may have been left in the jar.

Q Some fruits (especially pears, peaches, and apples) turn pink, red, blue, or purple when canned. Why?

A When fruit is heated, chemical changes take place that alter its color. There is no way to avoid this. It's harmless.

About jelly . . .

Q Why is my jelly too soft?

A The mixture may have had too much juice, too much acid, or too little sugar, or the mixture may not have been heated quickly enough.

Q Why is my jelly syrupy?

A The mixture may have had too little pectin or acid or the wrong amount of sugar (either too much or too little).

Q Why is my jelly too stiff?

A Either you used too much pectin, or fruit that wasn't ripe enough. Overcooking could also cause the problem.

Q If a jelly is cloudy, did it stand too long before being poured into the jars?

A Yes, this could be the cause. Or it might not have been strained well enough, the fruit might have been underripe, or it could have cooked too long.

Q Should I invert jelly glasses right after putting the lid on, as some books recommend?

A Inverting glasses gives a last heat treatment to the lids to kill all possible mold spores. Keeping lids scalding hot until they're used achieves the same results.

About pickles . . .

Q Why are my pickles hollow?

A Cucumbers may have been poorly developed or may have waited too long between harvesting and pickling; or fermentation may have been too quick because temperature was too high; or maybe the brine was too strong or too weak.

Q What is the white sediment in the bottom of the jar?

A If pickles are firm, it is only harmless lactic-acid bacteria that has grown and settled. If pickles are soft, it indicates spoilage and pickles shouldn't be eaten.

Q How can you prevent slippery pickles?

A Make sure you're using the correct amount of salt and vinegar. See that pickles are completely covered with liquid and that any scum is removed from brine before canning.

Q What causes pickles to turn dark?

A Minerals, such as iron, may have been present in the water or vinegar; or iron, zinc, copper, or brass utensils were used; or ground spices instead of whole spices were used; or pickles were heated too long.

About vegetables . . .

Q Is it dangerous if the liquid in the jars has turned cloudy?

A Yes, spoilage may have occurred; the food shouldn't be eaten (see "Guard Against Botulism," page 37, for information on how to dispose of spoiled food).

Q What is the white sediment in bottom of jars?

A It indicates starch or salts of acids from the vegetables or that hard minerals were present in the water. If water is cloudy, spoilage is indicated.

Q Must I sterilize glass jars and their lids before canning fruits and vegetables?

A **No**—not if you plan to use the water bath method or the steam pressure canning method in which both the containers and the food are sterilized during the processing at high heat. Just make sure jars, lids, and ring bands are clean, and that the lids are hot so they'll seal. **Yes**—if you're pickling without a canning kettle (see page 49) or making jams or preserves (see page 13). In both cases, make sure jars and lids are hot and clean.

FREEZING

Antidarkening agent: lemon juice, ascorbic acid, citric acid, or a combination of two in crystalline, powdered, or tablet form; used in solution to prevent browning of light-colored fruit.

Blanching: heating process that involves scalding vegetables in boiling water to slow down enzyme action.

Dry sugar pack: fruit packed for freezing with sugar.

Freezer burn: color, texture, and flavor changes in food, occurring in improperly wrapped packages.

Freezer paper: any type of coated or laminated paper used to wrap food for the freezer.

Freezer wraps: any type of coated or laminated freezer paper, heavy-duty foil, clear plastic wrap, or polyethylene sheets used to wrap food for the freezer.

Head space: unfilled space between food and lid that allows for expansion of food when frozen.

Liquid pack: fruit or vegetable packed for freezing in a liquid.

Moisture-vapor-resistant packaging materials: polyethylene bags and sheets, waxed or plastic laminated paper or boxes made especially for freezing, and various types of coated freezer papers.

Moisture-vaporproof packaging materials: glass jars, rigid plastic containers, heavy-duty foil, and clear plastic adhesive wrap.

Pectin pack: fruit packed for freezing in a syrup made from powdered pectin, sugar, and water.

Quick freeze: freezing food quickly by spreading on a baking sheet and placing in freezer. When frozen, food is packaged in large quantities; items remain loose, allowing for removing exact amount needed.

Syrup pack: fruit packed for freezing with a sweetened syrup.

Unsweetened pack: fruit packed for freezing without a sweetener or a liquid.

What happens in freezing?

Freezing is a great way to preserve the natural flavor of food. The trick is to freeze food fast and keep it at 0°F or below for long periods.

Food won't spoil as long as it stays solidly frozen at 0°F. That's because when foods freeze, the bacteria that cause spoilage (as well as the enzymes that cause further ripening) become inactive. When the foods thaw, the bacteria and enzymes become active again.

Freezing does produce some changes in food. The water in the food forms ice crystals that can puncture cell walls. The faster the freezing process, though, the smaller the ice crystals that form. When the food thaws, natural juices run out and the food can become mushy. Avoid partial thawing and refreezing—it increases cell damage and diminishes quality.

Even though food stored at 15° to 20°F may seem as solidly frozen as food at 10°F or below, it will be poorer in quality when thawed. This is the disadvantage of using the small freezer compartment of a refrigerator—it usually doesn't stay cold enough to keep food at 10°F or below, especially if there's heavy traffic in and out of the refrigerator. If the temperature of your freezer is above 10°F, use frozen foods within 2 months. To determine whether your freezer can accommodate longer storage periods, test its temperature with a mercury-type freezer thermometer.

Basic freezer information

Determine what size freezer to buy according to the size of your family, the productivity of your garden, your need to have extra food on hand, or the available space. Freezers come in a wide range of sizes, usually measured in cubic feet.

The manufacturer's booklet will tell you how much food you can freeze at any one time. The general rule is to freeze no more than 2 to 3 pounds of food at any one time for each cubic foot of freezer space. Adding more food than is recommended will increase the freezing time and raise the temperature of the food already frozen. When this happens, frozen food loses quality and may spoil. Also, place unfrozen food packages next to the freezing plates or coils in the coldest part of the freezer; leave enough space between the packages for the air to circulate. Once frozen, the packages can be stacked closer together.

Defrost your freezer periodically—built-up frost reduces storage space and raises the storage temperature. Though you can partially defrost your freezer often, you'll occasionally need to defrost it completely. When frost reaches a depth of ½ inch over a large area of the surface or begins to accumulate on packages stored only a few hours, it's time to defrost.

Choosing the right container

The way the food is packaged has a lot to do with its quality when thawed. Air inside a freezer container or package dries out frozen food and changes its color, texture, and flavor—changes known as *freezer burn.*

Protect frozen foods during storage by selecting a good-quality packaging material that is
• moisture-vapor-resistant;
• durable and pliable at low temperatures;
• certain not to impart flavor or odor to the food;
• resistant to absorbing water;
• easy to seal;
• suitable in size.

Glass, metal, and rigid plastic containers, heavy aluminum foil, and clear plastic adhesive wrap are moisture-vaporproof packaging materials. Since they prevent any moisture from penetrating the package, they provide the best protection for your food.

Polyethylene bags and sheets, waxed or plastic laminated paper or boxes made especially for freezing, and various types of coated or laminated freezer papers are sufficiently moisture-vapor-resistant to be satisfactory for freezing foods.

Rigid containers may be made of glass, metal, plastic, or heavily waxed cardboard and should have tight-fitting lids. Such containers are suitable for freezing whole fruit and liquid packs. Be sure to leave sufficient head space for expansion in all containers. You can use glass canning jars for freezing food not packed in water—water expands too much and would burst the jar.

Freezer bags, the most common of which are of transparent polyethylene, come in various sizes and are more suitable for vegetables, meats, and poultry than for fruits. You can use them for liquid packs, though they're not as convenient as rigid containers. Remember to press out any air and close the bags tightly by twisting the tops and tying them or by using rubber bands or twist ties.

Freezer wraps include heavy-duty foil, polyethylene sheets, clear plastic wrap, and the various types of coated or laminated freezer papers. Use them to wrap meat, fish, poultry, and large vegetables such as corn on the cob. Shape the wrap around the food to exclude as much air as possible. Seal the package with freezer tape. Paper with wax on one side is not recommended for freezer storage.

Thawing & refreezing

Some foods need no thawing before being cooked; others are best if partially or completely thawed. When a food needs to be thawed, leave it in its sealed package to prevent darkening and preserve the nutrients, especially vitamin C.

You can thaw food in the refrigerator, or at room temperature, or under running cold water. Thaw only enough for one meal—once thawed, the food should be used immediately.

When you refreeze food that's been partially thawed, you lose some of the quality. Consider food that is thawing as perishable until used.

You may safely refreeze partially thawed food if it still feels cold and contains ice crystals. For example, you can refreeze a 15-pound turkey that's been thawed for as long as 4 hours in the refrigerator. Use refrozen food as soon as possible.

If foods thaw over a period of several days to a temperature of 40°F, they are not good candidates for refreezing. And don't hesitate to discard any food that smells or tastes odd—it may contain harmful organisms.

What about power failures?

Brownouts and blackouts are common occurrences today. If you are warned ahead of time, immediately turn your freezer to the coldest setting—the lower the temperature, the longer the food will stay frozen.

A fully packed freezer will stay colder longer than a partially filled one. A full freezer will usually keep food frozen for 48 hours after a power failure; a half-filled freezer may not keep food frozen for more than 24 hours.

Adding dry ice to the freezer will help keep the food frozen longer. Add it as soon as possible after the power goes off. A 50-pound block should keep the food temperature in a 20-cubic-foot freezer below freezing for 3 to 4 days. If the freezer is half filled or less, it will remain below freezing for 2 to 3 days.

As you work, be sure your room is well ventilated for air circulation. Don't put ice directly on the packages, and don't touch it with bare hands; wear heavy gloves. Open the door only to take food out or to add more dry ice.

FREEZING FRESH FRUITS

Most fruits can be frozen, but one of the first things you'll want to consider is which varieties of a particular fruit freeze best. The chart on pages 84–85 tells you this. In all cases, be sure to choose fruit that's ripe, firm, and free from blemishes.

Remember to prepare only the amount of fruit your freezer can freeze within 24 hours (see manufacturer's booklet).

Is sugar necessary?

Some fruits can be packed with sugar or honey, or in a syrup; others need no sweetener at all.

If you want to eat the fruit raw when partially thawed or use it for pies or jams, you can freeze the fruit without a sweetener. This is referred to as *unsweetened pack*. The fruit is sliced or crushed in its own juice or, in some cases, frozen whole. But be aware that changes in color, flavor, and texture occur more rapidly than in fruits packed with a sweetener.

To add sugar before freezing, gently mix the sugar and fruit with a spatula until the fruit juices run out and the sugar is dissolved. The usual proportions are about one part sugar to four or five parts fruit measured by weight. This is referred to as a *dry sugar pack*. Using honey instead of sugar works only if your freezer stays at 0° F or below; at higher temperatures, the honey may crystallize.

(Continued on page 80)

Guide for Freezing Prepared Foods

Food	How to prepare and package	Freezer storage time	How to serve
Appetizers Sandwiches and canapés (fillings containing mayonnaise, sour cream, crisp vegetables, hard-cooked egg whites, and tomatoes not recommended for freezing)	Prepare as usual. Wrap individually or in small groups in freezer paper.	3 to 4 weeks	Arrange on serving trays and thaw at room temperature for about 1 hour.
Puff shells and crisp toast bases	Prepare bases and fillings. Do not combine. Spread separately in single layers on metal pans and freeze. Wrap tightly in freezer paper separately from other hors d'oeuvres.	3 to 4 weeks	Thaw in wrapping at room temperature for 2 to 3 hours. You may need to recrisp them in the oven before serving.
Stuffed olives and nuts, bacon-wrapped tidbits, and cheese rolls	Prepare as usual. Spread in single layers on metal pans and freeze. Package no more than 2 or 3 layers deep in shallow containers, separating layers with freezer paper.	2 to 4 months	Arrange on serving trays and thaw at room temperature for about 1 hour.
Dips and spreads containing cheese, ham and cold cuts, fish, avocado, and egg yolk mixtures (but *not* mayonnaise or sour cream)	Prepare as usual. Package in rigid containers.	2 to 4 months	Thaw at room temperature for about 1 hour.
Biscuits Baked	Prepare and bake as usual. Freeze; then wrap in freezer paper.	2 to 3 months	Heat without thawing in a 350° oven for 15 to 20 minutes.
Breads and rolls Quick breads (Gingerbread, nut and fruit breads, coffee cake, steamed breads)	Prepare as usual and bake until lightly browned. Cool quickly. Wrap in freezer paper or aluminum foil.	2 to 4 months	Thaw in wrapping at room temperature, or, if wrapped in foil, heat in a 400° oven. Slice fruit and nut breads while partially frozen to prevent crumbling.
Muffins	Prepare and bake as usual. Let cool. Package in freezer paper or in containers.	6 to 12 months	Thaw in wrapping at room temperature for about 1 hour, or heat in a 300° oven for about 20 minutes.
Waffles	Bake until lightly browned. Let cool. Wrap individually or in pairs in freezer paper.	1 to 2 months	Heat without thawing in a pop-up toaster, under the broiler, or on a baking sheet in a 400° oven for 2 to 3 minutes.
Yeast breads and rolls, baked (unbaked not recommended for freezing unless recipe is formulated for freezer storage)	Prepare and bake as usual. Cool quickly. Freeze; then wrap in freezer paper.	6 to 8 months	Thaw in wrapping at room temperature, or, if wrapped in foil, heat in a 300° oven for about 15 minutes for bread, 5 to 10 minutes for rolls.
Yeast breads and rolls (partially baked)	Prepare as usual. Bake in a 275° oven for about 20 minutes. Cool quickly. Wrap in freezer paper.	6 to 8 months	Thaw in wrapping at room temperature for 15 minutes. Bake in a

(Continued on next page)

Food	How to prepare and package	Freezer storage time	How to serve
Yeast breads (continued)			425° oven for 5 to 10 minutes or until lightly browned. If the bottoms of the rolls are too moist, bake on a wire rack instead of on a baking sheet.
Cakes Angel, chiffon, and sponge cakes	Prepare and bake as usual. Let cool. Do not use egg white in frosting. If frosted, freeze; then wrap in freezer paper. If unfrosted, wrap and freeze. Place whole cake in a box or carton to prevent crushing. To freeze slices, place a double fold of paper between slices. If tube pan has been used, fill hole in cake with crumpled freezer paper.	4 to 6 months	Thaw in wrapping on a rack at room temperature for 1 to 2 hours. Or, if unfrosted and wrapped in foil, heat in a 300° oven for 15 to 20 minutes. Thaw frosted cakes at room temperature or in refrigerator. Remove wrapping if frosting begins to stick to it.
Cheesecake	Prepare and bake as usual. Freeze; then wrap in freezer paper and store in a box.	4 months	Thaw unwrapped in refrigerator for 4 to 6 hours, or at room temperature for 30 minutes. If stored in a metal pan, dip bottom of pan in warm water to unmold.
Cupcakes	Prepare as usual, but bake in paper cups for easier storage. Freeze; then wrap individually or in pairs in freezer paper. Store in a box that can be opened easily to remove just the number to be used.	2 to 3 months	Thaw in wrapping at room temperature for about 1 hour, or, if unfrosted and wrapped in foil, heat in a 300° oven for 10 minutes.
Fruitcake	Prepare and bake as usual. Freeze; then wrap in freezer paper.	12 months	Thaw in wrapping at room temperature for about 1 hour per pound of cake.
Shortening cakes (including chocolate, nut, and spice)	Prepare and bake as usual. Let cool. Do not use egg white in frosting. (Frosting and cake are best frozen separately.) If frosted, freeze; then wrap in freezer paper. If unfrosted, wrap and freeze. Place whole cake in a box or carton to prevent crushing. To freeze slices, place a double fold of paper between slices.	2 to 4 months	Thaw in wrapping at room temperature for about 2 hours. Or, if unfrosted and wrapped in foil, heat in a 300° oven for 10 to 15 minutes for layer cakes, 25 to 30 minutes for loaf cakes. Thaw frosted cakes at room temperature or in refrigerator. Remove wrapping if frosting begins to stick to it.
Cookies Baked cookies	Prepare and bake as usual. Let cool. Package in cartons or plastic freezer bags with freezer paper between layers and crumpled in spaces.	6 to 8 months	Thaw in wrapping at room temperature for 15 to 20 minutes if cookies are crisp type. (They will be less crisp than cookies baked from frozen dough.) Place soft cookies on a serving plate to thaw.
Unbaked cookies (all types, except meringue)	For *refrigerator cookies*, form dough into roll. Slice, if desired. Wrap in freezer paper. For *drop cookies*, drop on a baking sheet, freeze, and package in a carton with freezer paper	6 months 6 months	Bake slices without thawing. Bake formed cookies without thawing in a 400°

Food	How to prepare and package	Freezer storage time	How to serve
Unbaked cookies (Continued)	between layers. Or prepare bulk dough and package in rigid container or in a plastic bag.		oven. Thaw bulk dough at room temperature until soft enough to drop by teaspoons on a greased baking sheet.
Creamed dishes (meat, fish, and poultry)	Prepare as usual. Slightly undercook added food. If waxy rice flour is available, use it to replace half or more of the flour. Omit hard-cooked eggs and cooked potatoes. Cool quickly by placing pan in running cold water or in ice water. Stir to hasten cooling, but don't beat in air. Package in rigid, wide-mouthed containers. Cover with a single thickness of freezer paper, cut to fit the surface. Leave head space. Lobster, crab, and shrimp will gradually toughen in storage.	Chicken—10 to 12 months Shellfish—1 to 2 months Other—4 to 6 months	Heat, frozen or thawed, in the top of a double boiler or in a 350° oven. If sauce has separated, stir until smooth.
Doughnuts	Raised doughnuts freeze best. Cake-type doughnuts may become slightly crumbly. Glazed doughnuts lose the glaze on freezing and thawing. Prepare all types as usual and let cool. Package in plastic freezer bags or in rigid containers with paper crumpled in spaces.	3 to 4 weeks	Thaw in wrapping at room temperature, or heat without thawing in a 400° oven until warm. Roll glazed doughnuts in granulated sugar, if desired.
Fish Baked fish	Prepare and bake as usual. Leave whole or in large pieces. Cool quickly by placing pan in running cold water or in ice water. Wrap in freezer paper, or in plastic freezer bags or rigid containers. If rigid containers are used, sauce or broth can be added. Be sure it covers fish, and fill spaces with crumpled freezer paper.	1 to 2 months	Heat without thawing in a 400° oven for 20 to 25 minutes.
Fish loaf	Prepare as usual. Pack in loaf pan but do not bake. Wrap in freezer paper, filling spaces with crumpled freezer paper, or place in a plastic bag.	1 to 2 months	Thaw in wrapping in refrigerator for 1 to 2 hours. Unwrap and bake in a 450° oven for 15 minutes; then reduce heat to 350° to finish baking.
Flaked fish (in sauce)	Prepare as usual, keeping fat to a minimum. Slightly undercook vegetables. Cool quickly by placing pan in running cold water or in ice water. Package in rigid, wide-mouthed containers. Be sure sauce covers fish. Leave head space.	4 to 6 months	Partially thaw in container at room temperature. Heat in the top of double boiler or in a 400° oven for about 30 minutes.
Fried fish pieces or sticks	Frozen fried fish may lose some fresh flavor and crispness; this is partly restored on reheating. Fry as usual, but do not completely cook. Cool quickly. Freeze on trays. Package in freezer paper or in plastic freezer bags.	1 to 2 months	Place frozen pieces or sticks in a single layer in a well-greased baking pan. Bake in a 400° oven for 20 to 25 minutes or until fish is crisp and heated through.
Frostings and fillings	Do not freeze fillings containing cream or eggs. Frosting containing egg whites becomes spongy. Frozen frostings lose their gloss; those with a lot of granulated sugar may become grainy. Cooked frostings may crack. Frostings containing confectioner's sugar freeze best. Package in rigid containers or in plastic freezer bags.	1 to 2 months	Thaw in container in refrigerator.
Gravy	Since gravy tends to separate and curdle when thawed, freeze broth and prepare gravy just before serving. To freeze gravy, add ¼ teaspoon unflavored gelatin to each quart of gravy to reduce curdling. Package in rigid containers.	2 months	Heat in the top of a double boiler, breaking up the frozen blocks.

(Continued on next page)

Food	How to prepare and package	Freezer storage time	How to serve
Macaroni, spaghetti, and other pasta	Usually better to cook just before using. If freezing is desired, undercook slightly. Package in cartons or in plastic bags.	1 month	Thaw in sauce or in a steamer for about 10 minutes.
Meat and poultry Fried meat and poultry	Frozen fried meat and poultry may lose some fresh flavor and crispness. Fry as usual until almost done. Cool quickly. Freeze on trays. Package pieces in freezer paper or in plastic freezer bags.	1 to 3 months	Thaw at room temperature. Place in a shallow pan and heat, uncovered, in a 350° oven for 30 to 45 minutes.
Roast meat and poultry	Roast as usual. Remove as much fat as possible. May be boned to save space, but keep pieces large. Turkey and other large birds should be cut off the bone to save space. Frozen ham and other cured meats often lose their color and become rancid more quickly than other meats. Sauce or broth helps keep meat from drying out and losing color. Package *dry meat* (for short storage) in freezer paper. Package *meat with sauce or broth* in rigid containers. Cover with sauce or broth. Cover with a piece of crumpled freezer paper. Leave head space.	2 to 4 months	Thaw dry meat in wrapping in refrigerator or at room temperature. Or place container in water. If wrapped in foil, heat in a 325° oven until heated through. Thaw meat with sauce in refrigerator for 5 to 6 hours, or heat slowly on top of range or in oven until heated through
Combination meat dishes (stews, spaghetti sauce with meat or meatballs, and ravioli)	Prepare as usual, keeping fat to a minimum. Omit potatoes from stew. Slightly undercook other stew vegetables. Cool meatballs and spaghetti sauce quickly by placing pan in running cold water or in ice water. Package in rigid, wide-mouthed containers. Be sure sauce or broth covers meat. Leave head space.	4 to 6 months	Partially thaw in container at room temperature. Heat in the top of a double boiler or in a 400° oven.
Meat loaf	Prepare as usual. Bake or leave unbaked.	3 to 4 months	To serve baked loaf cold, thaw in wrapping in refrigerator; to reheat place unthawed loaf in pan and bake in a 350° oven for 1 hour. Place unbaked frozen loaf in pan. Bake in a 350° oven for 1½ hours.
Nuts	Shell. Package in rigid containers or plastic freezer bags.	6 to 8 months	Thaw before using.
Pastry Baked pastry	Prepare and bake as usual. Let cool. Leave in pie pan or freeze before wrapping and remove from pan. Wrap in freezer paper, forcing out as much air as possible. Store in a box or carton to protect shells.	2 to 3 months	Thaw in wrapping at room temperature for 10 to 20 minutes. Add filling.
Unbaked pastry	Prepare pastry or crumb crust as usual. Fit into pie pans. Prick pastry. Stack pie pans with two pieces of freezer paper between each; then one crust may be removed at a time. Cover top pie crust with paper. Wrap stack with freezer paper. If desired, several flat rounds of pastry may be stored on cardboard and separated with two pieces of freezer paper between each one.	6 to 8 weeks	Bake in a 475° oven until lightly browned. Or, fill and bake as usual. If flat, place frozen pastry on pie pan until thawed and molded to pan.
Pies Chiffon pie	Make with gelatin base. Freeze before wrapping. Wrap in freezer paper or put in plastic bag. Store in carton.	2 weeks	Thaw in wrapping at room temperature for 1 hour.
Fruit, mince, and nut pies	Prepare as usual, adding 1 tablespoon flour or tapioca or ½ tablespoon cornstarch to very juicy fillings. This will help prevent fillings from boiling over when pies are baked. Do not cut vents in	Fruit and nut—3 to 4 months Mince—6 to 8 months	Without thawing, cut vent holes in upper crust. Place on cooky sheet. Bake in a 450° oven for

Food	How to prepare and package	Freezer storage time	How to serve
Fruit pies (Continued)	top crust. Do not bake. Steam and let light-colored fruits cool before making pie. For *apple pie*, dip raw apple slices in mixture of ½ teaspoon ascorbic acid to 1 cup water. For *peach pie*, peel peaches without scalding. Dip raw peach slices in mixture of 1 tablespoon lemon juice or ¼ teaspoon ascorbic acid to 1 cup water for each pie. Freeze fruit pies in their own pans. Wrap in freezer paper or put in plastic bags. Store in carton, or cover with empty pan turned upside-down and tape edges together.		15 to 20 minutes; then reduce heat to 375° and bake for 20 to 30 more minutes or until top crust is browned.
Pumpkin pie	Prepare pie shell and filling as usual. Cool filling before adding it to unbaked pie shell. Package the same as fruit pies.	4 to 5 weeks	Bake without thawing in a 400° oven for 10 minutes; then reduce heat to 325° to finish baking.
Fruit pie fillings	Prepare as usual. Freeze in rigid containers. Leave head space.	6 to 8 months	Thaw just enough to spread in pie crust.
Pizza	Prepare as usual. Do not bake. If topping is warm, let cool. Wrap in freezer paper.	1 month	Bake without thawing in a 450° oven for 15 to 20 minutes.
Potatoes French fries or shoestring potatoes	Cut strips rather small. Blanch or scald in boiling water for 1 to 2 minutes. Drain well. Fry quickly until lightly browned. Drain. Do not salt. Cool quickly. Package in rigid containers or plastic freezer bags.	2 to 3 months	Spread on a baking sheet. Heat without thawing in a 475° oven for 5 to 6 minutes, or fry in deep fat (watch carefully for spattering) until browned.
Salads	Fruit salads which are served frozen and have a base of cream or cottage cheese, whipped cream, or mayonnaise can be frozen. Do not freeze salads made with a separate gelatin layer, apples, grapes, or nuts. Fit a piece of freezer paper over top. Wrap in freezer paper.	6 to 8 weeks	Defrost in refrigerator for about 1 hour, and serve before completely thawed.
Sandwiches	Use day-old bread. Spread to edges with softened butter or margarine. Do not use crisp vegetables, hard-cooked egg whites, tomatoes, jellies, jams, or mayonnaise. Wrap individually or in groups in freezer paper. Sandwiches may be carefully wrapped in double thickness of wax paper if kept only a week or two. Store in carton or plastic freezer bag.	Cheese, ham, bologna—3 to 4 weeks Others—3 to 6 months	Thaw in wrapping at room temperature for 3 to 4 hours. Frozen sandwiches in a lunchbox will thaw in 3 to 4 hours and will help keep other food cool.
Dessert and meat Sauces	If flour is used in making sauce, see Gravy on page 77. Spices may change flavor over long storage; add them just before serving. Package in rigid container. Cover with crumpled freezer paper. Leave head space.	3 to 4 months	Thaw in container at room temperature, or heat in the top of double boiler. If sauce separates, stir well.
Soups and purées	Omit potatoes. If possible, make a concentrate by using less liquid when cooking. Vegetables may be cooked and puréed for use in cream soup. Cool quickly by placing pan in running cold water or in ice water. Package in rigid containers. Leave head space. Or freeze in ice cube trays, and store cubes in plastic bags.	4 to 6 months	Heat without thawing; heat cream soups in the top of double boiler. If cream soup has separated, stir until smooth. If concentrated, add hot liquid. Add potatoes or other vegetables, if necessary. Vegetable purée may be thawed in a covered casserole in a 400° oven or in a double boiler; then add cream or milk.

Mix fruit and sugar until juice is
drawn out and sugar dissolves

Another method for freezing fruit is in a *syrup pack*. Syrups used to pack fruit for freezing can be prepared in different concentrations. The following table gives you the proportions for making light, medium, and heavy syrups. Mix the ingredients until well blended.

SYRUP RECIPES

	YIELD	
Light syrup		
2 cups sugar and 4 cups water	5	cups syrup
1 cup honey, 1 cup sugar, and 4 cups water	5½	cups syrup
1 cup honey and 3 cups water	4	cups syrup
Medium syrup		
3 cups sugar and 4 cups water	5½	cups syrup
1 cup honey, 2 cups sugar, and 4 cups water	6	cups syrup
2 cups honey and 2 cups water	4	cups syrup
Heavy syrup		
4¼ cups sugar and 4 cups water	6½	cups syrup

Finally, you can pack some fruits—berries, peaches, peeled apricots, and cherries—in a *pectin pack*. Because less sugar is needed, the flavor and color are retained. Combine one package (1¾ oz.) powdered pectin with 1 cup water. Boil for 1 minute, stirring constantly. Stir in ½ cup sugar until dissolved. Remove from heat, add enough cold water to make 2 cups syrup, and refrigerate. Use instead of regular syrup.

Protecting fruit colors

Some light-colored fruits have a tendency to darken after they're cut; the chart on pages 84–85 specifies the treatment needed to preserve the color of those fruits.

To prevent darkening, either add an antidarkening agent to the syrup in which the fruit is packed or dissolve an antidarkening agent in water and sprinkle the liquid over the fruit before packing. When adding to the syrup, select a medium sweet syrup that makes about 5½ cups and add ½ to ¾ teaspoon ascorbic acid to it. Commercial antidarkening agents, usually containing ascorbic acid and citric acid (and often sugar), are available at supermarkets. Follow the manufacturer's directions.

Ascorbic acid crystals or powder are sold in drug stores. The typical addition is ½ teaspoon pure ascorbic acid powder per quart of light syrup. Ascorbic acid tablets can also be used, but they tend to make syrups cloudy. The tablets are more difficult to dissolve than the powder; crush them first. A total of 1,500 milligrams ascorbic acid tablets is needed for each quart of syrup.

Lemon juice can also be used as an antidarkening agent, but the quantity needed to prevent darkening can make the fruit too tart for your liking. (If you use Meyer lemons, double the amount of lemon juice called for.)

Packing fruit for the freezer

Select a container that protects the quality of the fruit while in the freezer. Rigid containers made of glass, metal, plastic, or heavily waxed cardboard work well. You can also freeze fruit in glass freezer jars or plastic freezer bags.

To pack fruit with syrup or sugar in wide-mouthed containers, leave ½ inch of head space at the top for pints and 1 inch for quarts. With narrow-mouthed containers, leave ¾ inch of head space for pints and 1½ inches for quarts. Crumple a piece of wax paper and place it on the top of

the fruit to hold the fruit under the syrup or juice. Then cover with the lid.

To pack fruit in soft containers such as plastic bags, exclude as much air as possible by submerging the bag of fruit in water up to the opening. When you seal the bags, make sure to leave the same head space as directed for narrow-mouthed containers—¾ inch for pints and 1½ inches for quarts. For other freezer containers, refer to the information on page 73.

Fruit Recipes

Fresh Fruit Ices

What's lighter than ice cream, cooler than sherbet, and packed with fresh fruit flavor? The answer is fresh fruit ices—and they're extremely simple to prepare, as well. Choose fruits and berries at the peak of their freshness, purée them, then freeze the purées until time to serve.

You'll need a food processor or blender to purée the fruit. Freeze the purée in divided ice cube trays; then tranfer the cubes to plastic freezer bags and return them to the freezer.

To serve, whirl in a food processor (using the metal blade) or in a blender until you have a velvety slush. Serve the ice at once in clear glass bowls that show off the sparkling natural color, or in shells made from half an orange, grapefruit, or pineapple.

Raspberry Ice. In a food processor or blender, whirl 4 cups **raspberries** until puréed. Pour through a sieve and discard seeds. Return purée to processor and add ¾ cup **sugar**, 1 tablespoon **lemon juice**, and ½ cup **water**. Whirl for 2 seconds. Freeze and serve according to preceding directions. Makes about 2¾ cups.

Lemon Ice. Remove zest (colored part of peel) from 1 small **lemon** and cut zest into ½-inch pieces. Place in a food processor or blender and add 1 cup **sugar**. Whirl until zest is finely chopped. Transfer to a 3-quart pan; add 4 cups **water** and a dash of **salt**. Heat just until sugar dissolves. Let cool, then stir in ⅔ cup **lemon juice**. Freeze and serve according to preceding directions. Makes about 4½ cups.

Orange Ice. From 1 **orange**, cut a ½ by 3-inch strip of zest (colored part of peel) into ½-inch pieces. Place in a food processor or blender and add ¾ cup **sugar**. Whirl until zest is finely chopped. Transfer to a small pan; add 1 cup **water** and heat just until sugar dissolves. Let cool, then stir in 1½ cups **orange juice** and 2 tablespoons **lemon juice**. Freeze and serve ac-

cording to preceding directions. Makes about 3 cups.

Frozen Fruit Yogurts

Here's a creamy dessert with the consistency of homemade ice cream but only half the calories—and at a fraction of the store-bought cost. You can make the yogurt mixture early in the day and store it in the refrigerator for several hours until you're ready to turn it in the ice cream freezer.

Fruit mixture (suggestions follow)
3 **eggs, separated**
¼ **teaspoon** *each* **salt and cream of tartar**
¼ **cup sugar**
2 **quarts unflavored yogurt (purchased or homemade)**

In a 3-quart pan over high heat, combine fruit and sugar (and honey, if used) for fruit mixture of your choice . Bring to a boil, stirring constantly. Reduce heat to medium and cook, stirring constantly, until fruit softens and partially disintegrates (1 to 4 minutes). Remove from heat; stir in fruit juices, spices, and flavoring as indicated for each fruit mixture.

In a small bowl, lightly beat egg yolks; stir in ½ cup of the hot fruit mixture. Then add egg yolk mixture to fruit mixture and stir well; cool to room temperature.

In a large bowl, beat egg whites until frothy. Add salt and cream of tartar, beating until soft peaks form. Gradually add the ¼ cup sugar and continue beating until stiff peaks form.

Place yogurt in a 5-quart or larger bowl; fold fruit mixture into yogurt until well blended. Then gently fold yogurt-fruit mixture into egg whites. (At this point, you may cover and refrigerate for several hours.)

Transfer mixture to a gallon-size or larger hand-crank or electric ice cream freezer. Assemble freezer according to manufacturer's directions, using about 4 parts ice to 1 part rock salt. When hand-cranking becomes difficult or when electric motor stalls, remove dasher. Transfer frozen yogurt to rigid plastic containers and place a piece of plastic wrap directly on top of frozen yogurt. Close container and freeze for at least 3 hours. Makes 1 gallon.

Fruit Mixtures

Apricot-orange. Use 4 cups thinly sliced unpeeled ripe **apricots**, 2 cups **sugar**, 2 tablespoons
(Continued on page 83)

4 cups pitted dark sweet cherries
1 cup sugar
1½ T cornstarch
2 T lemon juice
Pinch of salt
your favorite pie crust

drain the cherries to the juice
add the cornstarch lemon juice and

Cherries 6/80

Cherries 6/80

Cherr

lemon juice, ½ cup **orange juice,** 1 teaspoon grated **orange peel,** 4 teaspoons **vanilla.**

Banana-honey. Measure 4 cups thinly sliced ripe **bananas,** then coarsely mash. Use 1¼ cups **sugar,** ¾ cup **honey,** 3 tablespoons **lemon juice,** and 2 tablespoons **vanilla.**

Blackberry. Use 4 cups lightly packed whole fresh (or unsweetened frozen and thawed) **blackberries,** 2 cups **sugar,** and 4 teaspoons *each* **lemon juice** and **vanilla.**

Blueberry. Use 4 cups whole fresh (or unsweetened frozen and thawed) **blueberries,** 1¾ cups **sugar,** 2 tablespoons **lemon juice,** and 1 tablespoon **vanilla.**

Papaya. Coarsely mash enough peeled and seeded **papaya** (2 or 3 fruits) to make 2½ cups purée. Use 2 cups **sugar,** 2 teaspoons **vanilla,** and ¼ cup **lime juice.**

Peach. Use 4 cups sliced peeled **peaches,** 2 cups firmly packed **brown sugar,** 3 tablespoons **vanilla,** and ¾ teaspoon *each* **ground nutmeg** and **cinnamon.**

Raspberry. Use 4 cups lightly packed fresh (or unsweetened frozen and thawed) **raspberries,** 2 cups **sugar,** and 4 teaspoons *each* lemon juice and **vanilla.**

Frozen Yogurt Pops

Children will love this easy and nutrituous snack of fruit juice and yogurt. The flavor combinations are almost unlimited—pair your favorite fruit juice with unflavored or fruit-flavored yogurt.

Freezing the mixture in 3-ounce paper cups makes these yogurt pops easy and neat for youngsters to handle. Insert wooden sticks when the mixture is frozen enough to hold them upright. Then, when the pops are firm, simply peel off the paper cup and enjoy.

1 **can (6 oz.) frozen orange, grape, or apple juice concentrate**
1 **can (6 oz.) water**
1 **cup unflavored or fruit-flavored yogurt**
  Wooden popsicle sticks

Place juice concentrate, water, and yogurt in a blender or food processor. Whirl until well com-

bined. Pour even amounts into eight 3-ounce paper cups. Freeze partially, insert wooden sticks, then freeze until firm. Makes 8 pops.

Vanilla Custard Ice Cream
(Pictured on page 90)

One of the nicest ways to make ice cream is with fresh vanilla beans. Because the long, skinny, dark brown bean pod gives so little hint of its richly aromatic flavor, you may feel hesitant about using it—especially when you consider the simplicity of measuring out a spoonful of vanilla extract. But the difference in flavor is remarkable.

You'll find the pods in the spice section, labeled "vanilla bean."

> **3-inch piece of vanilla pod or 1½ teaspoons vanilla**
1½ **cups milk**
 1 **tablespoon cornstarch**
 ¼ **teaspoon salt**
 ¾ **cup sugar**
 4 **egg yolks, slightly beaten**
1½ **cups whipping cream**
  Ice
  Rock salt
1½ **cups chopped fruit (such as peeled peaches, strawberries, blueberries, or apricots), whirled in a blender or food processor (optional)**

Split vanilla pod, scrape beans into 2-quart pot, and drop in pod (or use vanilla extract). Add milk and bring to a boil over high heat, stirring occasionally.

Combine cornstarch, salt, sugar, and egg yolks; mix well. Beat a little of the scalded milk into egg mixture, then return mixture to pot, stirring. Cook over low heat, stirring constantly, until thick and smooth. Remove from heat, cover, and refrigerate until well chilled. Then remove vanilla beans and pods, and stir in cream. (At this point, you may cover and refrigerate until next day, if you wish.)

When ready to process, assemble hand-crank or electric ice cream freezer according to manufacturer's directions, using about 4 parts ice to 1 part rock salt. Pour ice cream mixture into cylinder (gallon-size or larger), cover, and begin cranking (or start motor).

If using fruit, add it about halfway through the processing, when ice cream has begun to thicken.

When hand-cranking becomes difficult or when motor stalls, remove dasher and let ice
(Continued on page 86)

Dark, tart Bing cherries may not be "as American as apple," but to many a connoisseur they rank high in pie-in-the-sky heaven. To can cherries, see chart on page 10; to freeze the pie (or several of them, while cherries are plentiful), see chart on pages 78 and 79.

Guide for Freezing Fruits

Fruit and varieties	Quantity to yield 1 pint	How to prepare
Apples Yellow Newtown Pippin, Golden Delicious, Jonathan, Rome Beauty, Gravenstein	1¼ to 1½ lbs.	**To pack in syrup,** put ½ cup cold medium syrup with ascorbic acid added into each container. Pare and core apples; slice directly into syrup. Press slices down and add syrup to cover fruit. Leave head space. **To pack in sugar,** wash, peel, and core apples. Slice directly into solution of 3 tablespoons lemon juice to 1 gallon cold water. After 2 to 3 minutes, remove slices and place on paper towels in refrigerator. Mix 1 part sugar with 4 parts apples. Place slices in plastic freezer bags or rigid containers. Leave head space.
Apricots Blenheim (Royal), Tilton	1 to 1¼ lbs.	Dip in boiling water; plunge into cold water; then peel. Cut in halves or quarters; remove pits. **To pack in syrup,** put ½ cup cold medium syrup with ascorbic acid added into each container; pack apricots. Add syrup to cover. Leave head space. **To pack in sugar,** sprinkle antidarkening solution over cut fruit; mix in ½ cup sugar per quart of fruit until sugar dissolves. Pack fruit and juice, pressing down until juice covers fruit. Leave head space.
Avocado Fuerte, Haas	4 medium	Peel, pit, and mash. Add 3 tablespoons lemon juice for each quart of purée. Pack in containers.
Berries raspberries, blueberries, elderberries, huckleberries, blackberries, boysenberries, loganberries	¾ to 1½ lbs.	Wash carefully in ice water; drain thoroughly. **To pack in syrup,** put berries in containers and cover with cold medium syrup. Leave head space. **To pack in sugar,** mix ¼ cup sugar to quart of raspberries; ½ cup sugar to quart of blueberries, elderberries, and huckleberries; ¾ cup sugar to quart of all other berries. Mix gently and fill containers. Leave head space. **To pack whole,** spread on baking sheet and quick freeze. Then transfer to rigid containers.
Cherries, sour or sweet Montmorency, Morello, Early Richmond,, Bing, Black Tartarian, Lambert, Royal Ann (Napoleon)	1 to 1½ lbs.	Pit, if desired (pits add flavor). **To pack in syrup,** put cherries in containers; cover with cold medium syrup with ascorbic acid added. Leave head space. **To pack in sugar,** combine cherries with ¾ to 1 cup sugar; mix until dissolved. Fill containers. Leave head space. **To pack whole,** leave stems on. Pack in containers.
Dates	1¼ lbs.	Wash, drain well, and pit if desired. Pack in containers.
Figs Black Mission, Kadota	¾ to 1¼ lbs.	Wash in ice water, remove stems, and peel. **To pack unsweetened,** pack in containers or cover with water, adding ¾ teaspoon ascorbic acid to 1 quart of water. Leave head space. **To pack in syrup,** pack in containers and cover with cold light syrup with ascorbic acid added. Leave head space.
Fruit purées and sauces		If necessary, cook or steam fruits in water until soft. Mash fruit, press through wire strainer, or whirl in a blender. Add sugar and/or lemon juice to taste. Heat to boiling; refrigerate. Pack in containers. Leave head space.
Grapefruit Marsh Seedless, Marsh Pink	2 lbs.	Wash and peel, cutting deep enough to remove white membrane under skin. Section; remove membranes and seeds. **To pack in syrup,** pack in containers and cover with cold light syrup (may be part fruit juice). Leave head space. Or freeze without syrup.
Grapes Muscat, Thompson Seedless, Ribier, Perlette, Cardinal, Red Malaga, Tokay	2 lbs.	Wash, place in containers (clusters or removed from stem). Make lemonade from frozen lemonade concentrate, decreasing water by 1 cup for each 6-ounce can. Pour over grapes until submerged. Leave head space. **To pack whole,** spread on baking sheet and quick freeze. Then transfer to rigid containers or plastic freezer bags.
Lemons and limes		Squeeze them and freeze juice in ice cube trays. Store in plastic freezer bags.

Fruit and varieties	Quantity to yield 1 pint	How to prepare
Mangoes Philippine, Hayden	2 to 3 medium	Wash, peel, and cut off slice at stem end. Slice. Avoid meat near seed. **To pack in syrup,** put ½ cup cold light syrup in each container; slice mangoes directly into syrup. Press slices down and add syrup to cover. Leave head space. **To pack in sugar,** place mango slices in a shallow bowl. Sprinkle with sugar, using 1 part sugar to 3 to 10 parts fruit by weight (½ cup to 5 to 6 cups mango slices). Let stand for a few minutes until sugar is dissolved. Mix gently. Pack in containers. Leave head space.
Melons cantaloupe, casaba, Crenshaw, honeydew, Persian, watermelon	1 to 1¼ lbs.	Peel and remove seeds. Cut in slices, cubes, or balls. **To pack in syrup,** put ½ cup cold light syrup in each container. Cut fruit directly into syrup; add syrup to cover. For flavor add 1 teaspoon lemon juice to each cup syrup. Leave head space.
Nectarines Early Sun Grand, Independence, Firebrite, Fairlane, Flavortop, Late le Grand	1 to 1½ lbs.	Peel as for apricots. Cut in halves or slices and remove pits. **To pack in syrup,** put ½ cup cold medium syrup with ascorbic acid added in each container. Cut halves or slices directly into cold syrup. Press fruit down and add syrup to cover. Leave head space.
Oranges any except Navel	3 to 4 medium	Wash and peel, cutting deep enough to remove white membrane under skin. Section; remove membrane and seeds. **To pack in syrup,** pack in containers and cover with cold medium syrup (may be part fruit juice). Or freeze without syrup. Leave head space.
Peaches Redtop, Rio Oso Gem, Fay Elberta, suncrest, O'Henry, Summerset	1 to 1½ lbs.	Peel as for apricots. Cut in halves or slices and remove pits. **To pack in syrup,** put ½ cup cold medium syrup with ascorbic acid added in each container. Cut halves or slices directly into syrup. Press fruit down and add syrup to cover. Leave head space.
Pears		Not recommended for freezing.
Persimmons freeze Hachiya as purée	1½ to 1¾ lbs.	**To pack whole,** dry fruit well after washing; remove stems. Spread on a baking sheet and quick freeze; then wrap each persimmon individually in foil or plastic freezer bag. To serve, hold frozen fruit under running cold water, peel, and eat while still frosty. Use within 3 months. **To freeze as purée,** see Fruit purées (at left).
Pineapple	4/5 lb.	Peel, remove core and eyes, cut into wedges, cubes, sticks, or thin slices, or crush. **To pack in syrup,** pack in containers and cover with cold light syrup. Leave head space.
Plums and fresh prunes Satsuma, Frontier, El Dorado, Late Santa Rosa, Queen Anne, French, Standard, Italian	1 to 1½ lbs.	Cut in halves and pit, or cut fruit away from pit in quarters. **To pack unsweetened,** leave plums whole; dry well after washing. Spread on a baking sheet and quick freeze; then pack in containers. Use cooked or in pies; use within 3 months. **To pack in syrup,** put ½ cup cold medium syrup with ascorbic acid added in each container. Press fruit down and add syrup to cover. Leave head space.
Rhubarb	⅔ to 1 lb.	Wash, trim, and cut rhubarb into pieces of desired length. Immerse in boiling water; after boiling resumes, cook for 1 minute. Drain; cool quickly in ice water and drain well. **To pack unsweetened** (or sprinkled with sugar), pack in containers. **To pack in syrup,** pack blanched rhubarb tightly in containers; cover with cold medium syrup. Leave head space.
Strawberries Tioga, Tufts, Sequoia, Pajaro, Douglas, Aiko	¾ to 1½ lbs.	Wash gently in cold water. Drain and hull. **To pack in sugar,** slice berries lengthwise or crush. Add ¾ cup sugar to 1 quart berries. Mix to dissolve sugar. Pack in containers. Leave head space. **To pack in syrup,** place whole or sliced berries in containers. Cover with cold medium syrup. Leave head space.
Tomatoes freeze as purée.	1¼ to 2¼ lbs.	Freeze only as sauce, paste, or purée (see Fruit purées, at left).

cream stand for about an hour (check manufacturer's directions). Then transfer to rigid plastic containers, laying a piece of plastic wrap directly on top of ice cream. Cover and freeze for at least 3 hours. Makes about 1½ quarts.

Vanilla Ice Milk

For a cold dessert that's not too rich, try this refreshing ice milk. You can make it with all milk or add a cup of cream to the milk mixture.

    3 eggs
    ¾ cup sugar
    ½ cup light corn syrup
    1½ tablespoons vanilla
    ⅛ teaspoon salt
    1 quart milk
    1 cup whipping cream (optional)

In a large bowl, beat eggs with a rotary beater. Stir in sugar and beat until thick and light colored. Mix in corn syrup, vanilla, and salt; continue beating until well blended. Stir in milk; add cream, if desired.

Pour mixture into a metal pan or into ice cube trays; cover and freeze for 1½ hours or until a 2-inch border has frozen. Transfer to a chilled bowl and beat with an electric mixer until fluffy. Cover and freeze until solid. Makes about 2 quarts.

Chocolate & Coffee Torte

This quick and easy freezer dessert never fails to win compliments. It's a perfect choice when you have very little time but must have something spectacular.

    1 cup macaroon cooky crumbs
    2 tablespoons butter or margarine, melted
    1 pint chocolate ice cream, slightly softened
    ½ cup chocolate-flavored syrup
    1 pint coffee ice cream, slightly softened
       About 4 ounces chocolate-covered hard toffee candy bars, coarsely chopped

Mix together cooky crumbs and butter; very lightly press into bottom of a 9-inch pie pan with removable bottom. Bake in a 350° oven for 8 to 10 minutes or until lightly browned. Let cool.

Spread chocolate ice cream evenly over cooled crust; drizzle with ¼ cup of the syrup and freeze until firm. Spread coffee ice cream evenly over top, sprinkle with crushed candy, and drizzle with remaining ¼ cup syrup. Cover and freeze until firm. Makes 6 to 8 servings.

Ice Cream Sandwiches

Who wouldn't find these chocolate-coated ice cream treats irresistible? You sandwich a slab of your favorite ice cream between chewy oatmeal cookies and then paint a thin layer of melted chocolate over all to conceal what's inside.

    ¾ cup solid vegetable shortening
    ½ cup granulated sugar
    1 cup firmly packed brown sugar
    1 egg
    ¼ cup water
    1 teaspoon vanilla
    1 cup all-purpose flour
    1 teaspoon salt
    ½ teaspoon baking soda
    3 cups rolled oats
    1 cup chopped nuts
    1 half-gallon ice cream (packed in rectangular carton)
    3 packages (6 oz. *each*) semisweet chocolate chips
    5 tablespoons solid vegetable shortening

In a large bowl, combine the ¾ cup shortening, granulated sugar, brown sugar, egg, water, and vanilla. With an electric mixer, beat until smooth. Add flour, salt, baking soda, oats and nuts; stir until well blended.

Grease two 10 by 15-inch rimmed baking pans. Spread half the batter evenly over bottom of one pan. Bake in a 350° oven for 12 minutes or until surface is just dry (*don't overbake*). Meanwhile, prepare second pan.

Remove from oven. Using a sharp knife and a ruler, immediately cut into 16 rectangles, each 2½ by 3¾ inches. Remove cookies from pan and let cool on wire racks. Meanwhile, bake second pan.

(Continued on page 88)

Teatime treats come fresh from a countertop toaster-oven (easy and safe for young cooks). Freeze rolled cooky dough as directed in chart on page 76. After it thaws slightly, kids can slice and bake.

To assemble, cut ice cream into 8 slices, each ½ to ¾ inch thick. Then cut each slice in half. Sandwich each slice between two cookies. Place on a baking sheet and freeze, uncovered, for about 4 hours or until firm.

Melt chocolate in top of a double boiler. Add the 5 tablespoons shortening and place over hot (*not boiling*) water; stir until mixture is melted and smooth. Chocolate becomes too thick if over-heated; to thin, remove from heat and stir for a few minutes until cooled.

Remove a few sandwiches from freezer at a time; if desired, trim off any uneven cooky edges. With a flat 1-inch paintbrush, coat edges with chocolate; then lay sandwiches on baking sheet and coat tops. Freeze, uncovered, for about 45 minutes or until firm.

Reheat chocolate by placing over hot water and stirring until melted. Turn frozen sandwiches over and coat remaining surface with chocolate. Freeze, uncovered, for 45 minutes or until firm. Wrap individually in plastic wrap or foil and store in freezer. Makes 16 sandwiches.

Frozen Soufflé with Strawberry Sauce

Two unusual ingredients—crushed macaroons and orange juice—contribute to the delicious flavor of this ice cream mold. Garnish with whole strawberries and pass sauce to spoon over individual servings.

⅓ cup chopped blanched almonds
1 quart vanilla ice cream
10 to 12 crisp macaroons, crushed
6 tablespoons orange juice
1 cup heavy cream, whipped
1 quart strawberries
2 teaspoons cornstarch
2 teaspoons water
½ cup sugar

Spread almonds in a shallow pan and toast in a 350° oven for 6 to 8 minutes or until lightly browned; set aside.

Let ice cream stand at room temperature until slightly softened. Transfer to a bowl; beat in crushed macaroons and 3 tablespoons of the orange juice. Fold in whipped cream. Spoon into a 1½-quart mold and sprinkle top with almonds. Cover and freeze until firm.

Wash strawberries and set aside 8 whole ones for garnish. Hull and slice remaining strawberries. In a pan, crush about half the sliced strawberries. Stir together cornstarch and water; add mixture to pan with sugar and remaining 3 tablespoons orange juice. Cook over medium heat, stirring often, until sauce is thickened. Add remaining sliced strawberries and let cool.

To serve, dip mold into very hot water for 10 seconds, then invert onto plate; garnish with reserved strawberries. Pass sauce at the table. Makes 8 servings

Easy Rainbow Sherbet Torte

Colorful scoops of sherbet create a rainbow effect in this easy freezer torte. To change the color and flavor, try using frozen yogurt or ice cream instead of sherbet.

1 pint orange sherbet
1 pint raspberry sherbet
1 pint lemon or lime sherbet
2 cups crisp coconut macaroon cooky crumbs
⅓ cup whipping cream or milk
½ cup chopped walnuts or toasted almonds

Let sherbets stand at room temperature to soften slightly while you prepare crust.

Measure ½ cup of the crumbs and set aside. Stir cream into remaining 1½ cups crumbs. Spread mixture lightly over bottom of a 9-inch round pan with removable sides.

Top crust evenly with spoonfuls of softened sherbet, alternating the three flavors to create a rainbow effect. Sprinkle reserved crumbs and nuts over top; press in gently. Cover pan with plastic wrap and freeze until firm—at least 8 hours or as long as 1 week.

To serve, remove torte from freezer about 30 minutes before you plan to serve, and let stand at room temperature. Remove pan sides. Cut torte into wedges. Makes 10 to 12 servings.

NO-COOK FREEZER JAMS

Frozen jams usually aren't as thick as traditional boiled jams, but they capture the fresh berry flavor and color of ripe fruit and also take less time to make.

When you make jams with two kinds of fruit, you get some intriguing new flavors. Try these recipes—you may become a convert to freezer jams. If you plan to use the jam within a month, you can keep it in the refrigerator. Otherwise, freeze it at a temperature of 10°F or below.

A word about pectin: two brands of powdered pectin are available. The packages vary in ounces. Be sure to use the amount specified in the recipe.

Fresh Strawberry Jam

4 cups fully ripe strawberries, hulled
1 package (2 oz.) powdered pectin
1 cup light corn syrup
5½ cups sugar
4 tablespoons lemon juice

Crush strawberries to make about 8 cups and place in a 2-quart pan. Stirring vigorously, slowly sift in powdered pectin. Let stand for 20 minutes, stirring occasionally to dissolve pectin completely. Pour in corn syrup and mix well. Gradually stir in sugar. When sugar is thoroughly dissolved, stir in lemon juice.

Ladle jam into 8 sterilized half-pint jars, cover, and freeze for at least 24 hours. (The jam won't be solid because of the sugar concentration.) Makes 8 half pints.

Fresh Peach Jam

2 cups peaches, peeled and thinly sliced
3 tablespoons lemon juice
4 cups sugar
1 package (1¾ oz.) powdered pectin
1 cup water

In a heatproof bowl, combine peaches and lemon juice. With a fork or pastry cutter, crush fruit. Stir in sugar and let stand for about 20 minutes, stirring occasionally.

In a small pan, combine pectin and water. Bring to a boil and boil for 1 minute, stirring constantly. Pour hot pectin mixture over peaches; stir for 2 minutes. Pour into 4 or 5 sterilized half-pint jars, cover, and let stand at room temperature for about 1 hour or until jam is set. Refrigerate for up to 3 weeks; freeze for longer storage. Makes 4 or 5 half pints.

Strawberry-Raspberry Jam

2⅔ cups crushed strawberries
1⅓ cups crushed raspberries
1 package (2 oz.) powdered pectin
1 cup light corn syrup
5½ cups sugar
2 tablespoons lemon juice

Place crushed strawberries and raspberries in a 3-quart pan. Stirring vigorously, slowly sift in powdered pectin. Let stand for 30 minutes, stirring occasionally to dissolve pectin completely. Pour in corn syrup and mix well. Gradually stir in sugar. Carefully heat mixture to 100°F (it should be lukewarm and no hotter). When sugar is thoroughly dissolved, stir in lemon juice. Ladle into 8 sterilized half-pint jars, cover, and freeze for at least 24 hours. Makes 8 half pints.

Strawberry-Apple Jam. Follow preceding instructions, substituting 3¼ cups crushed **strawberries** and ¾ cup **apple juice** for the 4 cups crushed berries.

FREEZING VEGETABLES

Home vegetable gardens of every shape and size thrive all over these days—from large urban areas to more rural surroundings. If you're one of those fortunate gardeners with more fresh vegetables than you can use or give away, consider harvesting part of your crop for freezing.

Successful home freezing depends on absolutely fresh vegetables. Here the home gardener has a distinct advantage—he or she can pick vegetables at their peak of maturity and freeze them without delay. To determine the best time to pick your crop, see "Home Harvesting," pages 114–115.

Freezing vegetables successfully and being able to keep them frozen for more than just a few weeks depends on the type of freezer you have. You need a freezer that stays at 0°F or lower without any dramatic fluctuations. The freezer compartment of most refrigerators does not meet these requirements.

Low temperatures allow vegetables to freeze quickly with minimal deterioration in texture. For more information, see "'Basic freezer information," page 73.

Most vegetables need to be heated by a process called *blanching* before they can be packaged for freezing. Blanching involves scalding the vegetables in boiling water for a few minutes to slow down the enzyme action and retard the spoiling process. This preserves the vegetable's color, flavor, texture, and nutritive value. Follow the blanching times given for each vegetable on the chart on pages 92–93. Use the shorter times for small, young vegetables, the longer times for more mature vegetables or those cut in larger

pieces. Add 1 minute to the blanching time if you live 5,000 feet or more above sea level.

To blanch, place no more than 2 pounds of vegetables at a time in a wire basket, metal colander, or cheesecloth bag. Immerse in a large pot of rapidly boiling water. When the water returns to a boil, cover the pot and start counting the blanching time. If the water takes more than 2 minutes to resume boiling, use fewer vegetables next time. Immediately chill blanched vegetables by plunging the basket into ice water or holding it under cold running water until the vegetables are completely cold.

Immediately cool blanched
vegetables under cold running water

Protecting vegetable colors

Some vegetables, like some fruits, require treatment to prevent darkening; the chart on pages 92–93 specifies the treatment needed for those vegetables. The antidarkening agent—citric acid (available in drugstores) or lemon juice—is added to the blanching water. The chart directs how much to use; remember to double the amount of lemon juice if you're using Meyer lemons.

Packing vegetables for the freezer

You can package vegetables in many types of freezer containers. Loose vegetables, such as cut green beans, chopped broccoli, and mushrooms, are usually packed in plastic freezer bags and then placed in cardboard freezer cartons; the cartons make stacking easier and protect the bags

(Continued on page 94)

Summertime is ice cream time—and full of sweet memories when you crank up the ice cream at home. Starting with fresh vanilla custard, you can move on to experiment with summery fruit flavors. The recipes are on page 83.

Guide for Freezing Vegetables

Vegetables	Quantity to yield 1 pint	How to prepare
Artichokes	20 to 25 1¼″ artichokes	**For whole medium-size artichokes,** pull off coarse outer leaves; cut 1″ off tops; trim tips and stems. Wash. Blanch for 10 minutes, adding 3 teaspoons citric acid or ½ cup lemon juice to 2 quarts water. Chill. Pack in plastic freezer bags. **For artichoke hearts,** cut off top third of small artichokes; trim all but ½″ of stems. Pull off all leaves down to edible pale leaves. Blanch for 3 to 5 minutes, adding citric acid or lemon juice as for whole artichokes (see above).
Asparagus	1 to 1½ lbs.	Cut off tough ends of stalks. Sort according to size. Wash. Blanch for 2 to 4 minutes. Chill. Pack in plastic freezer bags.
Beans, lima	⅔ to 1 lb.	Wash and snap off ends. Cut into 1″ pieces or cut lengthwise. Blanch for 2 to 3 minutes. Chill. Pack in plastic freezer bags.
Beans, string, wax, and Italian	2 to 2½ lbs.	Hull and wash beans; sort according to size. Blanch for 2 to 4 minutes. Drain and chill. Pack in plastic freezer bags.
Beets	1¼ to 1½ lbs.	Remove tops. Wash and peel. Leave whole if small, or slice or dice. Blanch for 3 to 5 minutes. Chill. Pack in plastic freezer bags.
Broccoli	1 lb.	Trim outer leaves and wash. Cut large stalks into ½″-thick pieces. Sort according to size. Blanch for 3 to 4 minutes. Chill. Pack in plastic freezer bags.
Brussels sprouts	1 lb.	Trim, remove outer leaves, and wash. Sort according to size; blanch for 3 to 5 minutes. Chill. Pack in plastic freezer bags.
Cabbage	1 to 1½ lbs.	Discard outside leaves. Cut heads into convenient-size pieces. Blanch for 3 to 4 minutes. Drain and chill. Pack in plastic freezer bags.
Carrots	1¼ to 1½ lbs.	Remove tops. Wash and scrape. Use small, tender carrots whole; dice or slice others into ½″ pieces. Blanch for 2 minutes for slices, 5 minutes for whole. Chill. Pack in plastic freezer bags.
Cauliflower	1¼ lbs.	Break into 1″ pieces. Wash. Blanch for 3 minutes, adding 1 tablespoon vinegar to 1 gallon water. Chill. Pack in plastic freezer bags.
Celery	1 lb.	Trim crisp stalks. Wash thoroughly and cut into 1″ lengths. Blanch for 3 minutes; cool in ice water and drain. Pack in plastic freezer bags.
Chayote	1½ to 2 lbs.	Wash, remove stem and blossom ends. Do not peel. Dice. Blanch for 2 minutes; cool in ice water and drain. Pack in plastic freezer bags.
Corn	2 to 3 lbs. (6 to 8 ears)	Husk, remove silk, and wash. Sort for size. **For kernels,** blanch whole ears for 4 minutes; cool quickly; cut kernels from cob. Chill. Pack in plastic freezer bags. **For corn on cob,** pierce cob lengthwise with a sharp knife; blanch for 3 to 4 minutes; chill very thoroughly. Wrap in heavy-duty foil, or pack in plastic freezer bags.

Vegetable	Quantity to yield 1 pint	How to prepare
Eggplant	1 to 1½ lbs.	Wash, peel, and cut into strips ½ by 2″ or dice. Blanch for 2 to 4 minutes; let cool. Prevent darkening by dipping in mixture of 1 tablespoon citric acid or ½ cup lemon juice and 5 cups water. Drain well. Pack in plastic freezer bags.
Ginger root	1 whole piece	Wash well and dry. Do not blanch. Wrap whole in freezer paper. **To use,** grate or slice unthawed root. Return unused portion to freezer.
Greens spinach, Swiss chard, beet greens	1 to 1½ lbs.	Wash to remove sand and grit; cut off heavy stems. Blanch leaves for 1½ minutes, stirring well. Chill and drain. Pack in plastic freezer bags.
Kohlrabi	1¼ to 1½ lbs.	Use firm, small roots 2 to 3″ in diameter. Cut off and discard tops. Wash, peel, and dice. Blanch for 1½ minutes. Cool quickly and drain. Pack in plastic freezer bags.
Mushrooms	1 to 2 lbs.	Wash thoroughly. Trim stems. Leave whole or slice. Blanch for 2 to 4 minutes (depending on size), adding 1 tablespoon lemon juice to 1 quart water. Or cook in butter until tender. Chill. Pack in plastic freezer bags.
Okra	1 to 1½ lbs.	Wash, cut off stems, but don't open seed cells. Blanch small pods for 3 minutes; large pods for 4 minutes. Cool in ice water; drain. Leave whole or slice crosswise. Pack in plastic freezer bags.
Onions yellow, white	1 to 3 whole	Peel and chop. Do not blanch. Freeze in small freezer bags. Use within 2 months.
Parsnips	1¼ to 1½ lbs.	Cut off tops and wash thoroughly in running cold water. Peel. Cut into ½″ cubes or slices. Blanch for 2 minutes. Cool in ice water for 5 minutes; drain. Pack in plastic freezer bags.
Peas	2 to 3 lbs.	Shell peas, wash. Blanch for 1½ minutes. Pack in plastic freezer bags.
Peppers, bell green and red	1 to 3 lbs.	Wash, remove stem and seeds. Cut in halves or slices. Do not blanch. Pack in small containers for convenience.
Potatoes, new	2 to 4 lbs.	Cook until barely tender. Chill. Pack in plastic freezer bags. Thaw in bags when ready to use.
baked and stuffed		Bake and stuff as usual; let cool. Wrap individually in foil and freeze. Then place in plastic freezer bags or heavy-duty foil.
Rutabaga	1¼ to 1½ lbs.	Cut off tops, peel, and dice. Blanch for 1 minute. Cool quickly and drain. Pack in containers.
Snow peas	⅔ to 1 lb.	Remove stem and blossom ends and any string. Blanch for 1½ minutes. Chill. Pack in plastic freezer bags.
Spinach		See Greens.
Squash, summer crookneck, pattypan, zucchini	1 to 1¼ lbs.	Wash and cut off stem ends. Cut into ½″ slices. Blanch for 3 minutes. Chill. Pack in containers.
Squash, winter banana, butternut, Hubbard, pumpkin	1 to 1½ lbs.	Wash and peel. Cut open and remove seeds, cut into chunks. Cook until soft in a small amount of water, then mash; let cool. Pack in rigid containers.
Tomatoes		See Guide for Freezing Fruits, page 85.
Water chestnuts		Unused portions of canned water chestnuts may be frozen. Pack in small plastic freezer bags.

from tearing. Wrap corn on the cob in heavy-duty foil or freezer wrap. Rigid containers, such as plastic boxes with tight-fitting lids or glass freezing jars, are convenient for packing solid vegetables like cooked winter squash.

No matter what container you use, it's important to exclude as much air from it as possible. For a plastic bag, submerge the bag in water up to the opening to force out air; then press the bag against the food. Vegetables expand as they freeze, so leave ½ inch of head space for soft containers and 1 inch for rigid containers. Seal well—twist wire ties on plastic bags, attach lids on plastic boxes, screw ring bands dowen tightly over lids on glass freezing jars. Label all containers with the type of food and the date; freeze immediately.

Vegetable Recipes

Fresh Marinara Sauce

(Pictured on page 39)

Because home-grown tomatoes often ripen faster than you can eat them, you'll appreciate this versatile, well-seasoned tomato sauce that can be made and frozen. Though you can use any variety of tomatoes, or a combination of varieties, pear-shaped tomatoes are preferred because they're meatier and less watery.

- 6 **pounds (about 15 medium-size) pear-shaped or other ripe tomatoes Boiling water**
- ⅓ **cup olive oil or salad oil**
- 6 **cloves garlic, pressed or minced**
- 2 **large onions, chopped**
- 3 **or 4 large carrots, finely chopped**
- 2 **tablespoons dry basil or ⅓ cup finely chopped fresh basil**
- 1 **tablespoon oregano leaves or 3 tablespoons finely chopped fresh oregano**
- 2½ **teaspoons salt**
- ¾ **to 1 teaspoon pepper**

Immerse tomatoes, a few at a time, in boiling water for about 1 minute. Lift out with a slotted spoon and plunge into cold water. Peel off and discard skins. Coarsely chop tomatoes to make 11 to 12 cups total.

Heat oil in a 5-quart or larger pot over medium heat. Cook garlic, onions, and carrots, stirring occasionally, until soft. Stir in tomatoes, basil, oregano, salt, and pepper. Bring to a boil. Reduce heat and simmer rapidly, uncovered and

stirring occasionally, for about 1½ hours or until sauce is very thick and reduced by about half.

Let cool. Pour into freezer containers, cover, and freeze for up to 4 months. Makes 1½ to 2 quarts.

Marinara Sauce with pasta. Cook about 8 ounces **spaghetti** or other pasta according to package directions; drain well. Spread on a platter and mix with about 4 cups hot **marinara sauce**. Sprinkle with chopped **parsley** and serve with grated **Parmesan** or Romano **cheese**. Makes 6 first-course servings.

Marinara Sauce with beef or shellfish. Spoon hot **marinara sauce** over individual servings of broiled **steak** or ground beef patties or servings of hot cooked **scallops**, cold crab, or boiled or broiled shelled and deveined shrimp. Allow about 2 cups sauce for 4 servings.

Marinara Sauce with vegetables. Heat 1 cup **marinara sauce** with 1 tablespoon chopped **parsley**. Stir into 1 pound hot cooked whole **green beans** or 1¼ pounds hot cooked sliced **zucchini**. Sprinkle with 3 tablespoons toasted **pine nuts**. Makes 4 servings.

Caponata

(Pictured on page 47)

This version of caponata, a thick, piquant mixture made primarily with cooked eggplant, comes from Sicily. As a first course or as part of an antipasto platter, spread it on crackers, or spoon it on crisp lettuce leaves and accompany with slices of crusty bread.

- ½ **cup olive oil**
- 2 **cups diced celery**
- 1 **medium-size eggplant (unpeeled), cut into ¾-inch cubes**
- 1 **large onion, chopped**
- ⅓ **cup wine vinegar**
- 1 **teaspoon sugar**
- 2 **large tomatoes, peeled and diced**
- 1 **cup water**
- 1 **tablespoon capers, drained**
- ¼ **cup sliced pimento-stuffed Spanish olives**
- 1 **can (2¼ oz.) sliced ripe olives, drained**
- 2 **tablespoons minced parsley Salt**

(Continued on page 96)

Fresh from this morning's catch, cleaned trout await quick freezing to capture their flavor at its peak. To freeze fish, see page 99.

... Caponata (cont'd.)

Heat oil in a wide frying pan over medium heat. Add celery and cook, stirring, until tender. With a slotted spoon, remove celery and set aside.

Add eggplant to pan and cook, stirring, over medium heat until lightly browned and tender enough to mash easily. Add onion and continue cooking and stirring until onion is soft but not browned. With a slotted spoon, remove eggplant and onion.

Add vinegar, sugar, tomatoes, and water to pan. Cook, stirring, over medium heat for 5 minutes. Return celery, eggplant, and onion to pan. Stir in capers, Spanish and black olives, and parsley until will blended. Reduce heat and simmer, uncovered, for about 20 minutes. Add salt to taste.

Remove from heat and let cool. Serve at room temperature. Or cover and refrigerate for up to 1 week. To freeze, place in plastic freezer bags, glass freezer jars, or plastic containers and store for up to 4 months. Makes about 2 quarts.

FREEZING MEAT, POULTRY & SEAFOOD

A cache of meat, poultry, or seafood on hand in the freezer is a welcome sight for a busy cook, as well as a boon to the food budget. Keep an eye out for bargains on whole chickens or sides of beef—a freezer allows you to take advantage of these specials.

Buying meat for freezing

You can purchase whole carcasses, sides, or quarters of meat wholesale or on sale in retail markets. The *wholesomeness* of your meat is guaranteed if it bears the round, purple United States Department of Agriculture (USDA) inspection stamp. The *quality* of the meat—

tenderness, juiciness, and flavor—is indicated by the shield-shaped USDA grade mark. Do not confuse the two marks.

When you purchase a whole carcass or side (half a carcass) of beef, you get a wide range of cuts, some of which you may not want. An alternative is to select just the cuts you're certain you'll use, buying from either wholesale or retail sources. When you buy a whole carcass or side, you're paying for the untrimmed weight. Once trimmed, figure on losing about 25 percent of the poundage you purchase. A good rule of thumb is 25 percent steaks, 25 percent ground beef and stew meat, 25 percent roasts, and 25 percent waste. A hindquarter of beef will yield more steaks and roasts as well as more usable lean meat than the forequarter, but will cost more per pound.

Buying lamb is easier than buying beef because the quality of lamb is less variable. Lamb is produced from animals less than a year old.

The United States Department of Agriculture grades pork as either acceptable or unacceptable. Retail markets handle only acceptable grades. It's wisest to buy a whole pork carcass from an establishment that can render the lard and cure the bacon, hams, and other cuts that you may not want to use fresh. If you can't have this done, just buy wholesale cuts of fresh pork and hams; look for cuts with small amounts of fat over the outside and firm, grayish pink meat.

The amount of meat you buy for the freezer depends on your available freezer space, your family's needs, your budget, and the amount your freezer can freeze at any one time (see manufacturer's booklet).

It's usually best to have the meat market freeze large meat purchases, since all the meat needs to be frozen at once.

Freezing batches slowly at home can cause formation of large ice crystals, which breaks down the cells; when the meat is thawed, more juices are lost.

Preparing meat for the freezer

You can lay to rest two common misconceptions about freezing: it neither tenderizes nor sterilizes meat. What it does do is to make most enzymes inactive and kill some of the bacteria and molds normally present in meat.

When you're cutting the meat yourself for freezing, start by making sure all utensils and cutting boards are spotlessly clean. First chill the carcass; then cut it into pieces. To save freezer space, trim off excess fat before wrapping, and bone pieces with a high percentage of bone.

Package the meat in heavy-duty foil, polyethylene sheets, or coated or laminated freezer paper. Wrap the meat closely, eliminating all air, if possible. Place a double thickness of wax paper between chops and steaks so they won't stick.

There are two techniques for wrapping meat for the freezer—drugstore wrap and butcher wrap. A drugstore wrap is like wrapping a package. Place meat in the center of the paper, using enough paper so both edges can fold down two or

Fold edges together 2 or 3 times, bringing paper tight against meat

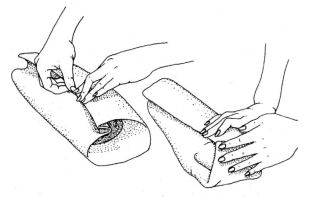

Fold ends down, then tightly back up against package

three times. Bring the two edges of paper together above the meat and make a fold. Fold down in ½ to 1-inch folds until the paper is tight against the meat. Press out as much air as possible at each end. Fold ends down tightly against the package. Secure the package with freezer tape.

Start in corner of paper; fold edges over and against meat

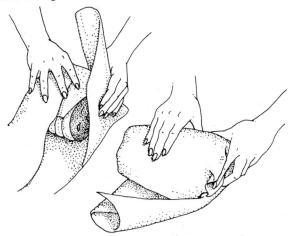

Roll package over and over until paper is used

To butcher wrap, place the meat close to one corner of the paper. Fold a corner against the meat and the side of the paper over the meat. Roll the package over and over until all the paper is used. Secure with freezer tape.

Remember to label the packages with the cut of meat, the weight or number of servings, and the date.

Freeze meat quickly at 10°F or below, with space left for air circulation between the packages. Properly wrapped meat, stored at 0°F or below, will keep its quality for a long time.

Though it's safe to refreeze meat that has been partially thawed in refrigerator, you can expect a loss of quality.

The chart below lists suggested storage time for meat at 0°F.

BEEF

Ground	3 to 4 months
Pieces and cubes	6 to 8 months
Roasts and steaks	8 to 12 months

LAMB

Ground	3 to 4 months
Roasts and chops	8 to 12 months

PORK

Ground sausage	1 to 3 months
Roasts and chops	6 to 8 months
Smoked pork and ham	1 to 3 months

Preparing poultry for the freezer

Chickens, ducks, geese, and turkeys can be frozen whole, halved, quartered, or in pieces. Never stuff poultry before freezing—the stuffing takes so long to cool inside the bird during freezing, and to thaw and reheat during roasting that food spoilage and bacteria growth can take place. This could result in food poisoning.

To freeze whole birds, wrap and freeze giblets separately, for they develop an odd flavor in about 3 months, If you plan to use the poultry within 3 months, you can wrap the giblets in freezer paper and tuck them into the body cavity. Tie the leg ends of the cleaned bird together; press the wings close to the body or tuck them back akimbo-style.

Place the bird in the center of a sheet of freezer paper; bring the long sides over the bird, and fold together about 1 inch of the edges. Fold again to bring the paper tight and flat over the bird. Force out air by pressing the wrapping close to

(Continued on page 99)

the bird. At each end, fold the corners toward each other, making a tight package.

You can also package poultry in plastic bags, pressing out as much air as possible before fastening bags. Submerge the bag in water up to the opening, and press the bag against the poultry to expel air.

To freeze poultry halves, package them together with a double thickness of freezer paper between them, or wrap them separately.

To freeze pieces of poultry, separate the meaty pieces from the bony ones (use the bony pieces in soup). Place meaty pieces close together in a plastic freezer bag or carton, or wrap in freezer paper, separating pieces with two sheets freezer paper to hasten thawing. (Darkening near the leg bones is caused by the seepage of blood from the bone marrow during freezing, thawing, and cooking—the quality of the meat isn't affected.)

Store poultry at 0°F for 6 to 12 months.

Preparing seafood for the freezer

To keep well, fish must be kept cold after being caught, then quickly cleaned and frozen. Freeze small fish whole; cut large fish into steaks, fillets, or boned strips before freezing.

To prevent fatty fish such as tuna and salmon from darkening and becoming rancid, dip pieces in an ascorbic acid solution (made with 2 tablespoons ascorbic acid to 1 quart water) for 20 seconds. Then package the fish in freezer wrap in meal-size portions, separating pieces with a double thickness of freezer wrap. Freeze quickly and store at 0°F.

Shellfish can be frozen easily. For shrimp, remove the heads but do not shell. Rinse shrimp in a solution of 1 teaspoon salt to 1 quart water. Drain well, package in freezer containers, and freeze. Store at 0°F.

Clams and oysters should be shucked or opened and placed in a colander to drain; reserve juices. Remove and wash meat thoroughly and quickly in a solution of 1 tablespoon salt to 1 quart water; drain well. Package meat in glass freezer jars or other freezer containers; cover with reserved juices, leaving about ½-inch head space. Freeze quickly and store at 0°F.

For crab, break off claws and legs. Remove back shell, gills, crab butter, and other viscera. Wash pieces well and cook as soon as possible. Steaming the crab for 15 to 20 minutes will preserve color and flavor. Cool slightly, then pick meat from body and legs while still warm. Tightly pack in glass freezing jars or other freezer containers, removing as much air as possible. If you plan to store crab for more than 4 months, cover meat with a solution of 3 tablespoons salt mixed with 1 gallon water; leave ½-inch head space in container. Freeze quickly and store at 0°F.

To freeze crab in its shell, carefully package each crab in freezer wrap or in a rigid container, preferably in an ice-salt mixture (8 parts crushed ice to 1 part salt). Though the meat will discolor, it will still have a good flavor.

The chart below lists suggested storage times for seafood at 0°F.

FISH

Fatty fish (tuna, salmon)	1 to 3 months
Lean fish (haddock, sole, trout)	4 to 6 months

SHELLFISH

Crab and lobster	1 to 2 months
Oysters	1 to 3 months
Clams and scallops	3 to 4 months
Shrimp	4 to 6 months

For more information about freezing, write for Bulletin #93, "Freezing Meat & Fish in the Home" from the U.S. Department of Agriculture, Washington, D.C.

Freezing fresh herbs

Freezing is a good way to preserve the fresh, more tender herbs such as basil, dill, chives, and tarragon. Simply wash freshly picked herbs, carefully pat dry, and freeze in small plastic freezer bags, foil, or freezer paper in amounts you might use at one time. Because frozen herbs will darken and become limp when thawed, add them directly from the freezer to the food you are cooking.

In lacy dried bouquets, herbs please the eye as positively as they please the palate. Set a few decorative bundles aside after drying and storing portions to be used in cooking (directions are on page 125). Here a purchased bay wreath hangs over pots in the background. Adorning the doorway are a garlic-shallot braid (also purchased) and a clutch of red peppers. Suspended in the foreground, clockwise from top, are bundles of sage, basil, rosemary, thyme, and marjoram.

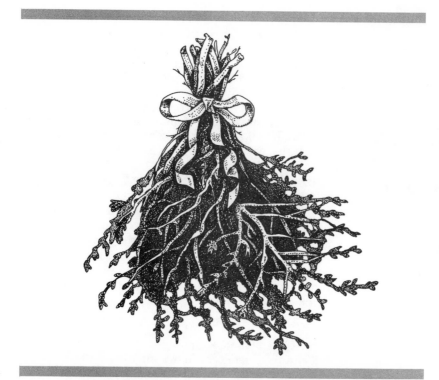

DRYING

What happens in drying?

There is nothing new about food drying. It's perhaps the oldest form of food preservation, dating back to earliest civilizations. Of course, more sophisticated techniques are used today, but the general principle of removing moisture from food by exposing it to temperature increases and moving air hasn't changed.

To dry or dehydrate any type of food, you must control both the temperature and the circulation of air around the food in order to prevent spoilage. Many different methods may be used, but whatever the method, if the temperature is too low or the humidity too high, the result is that food will dry too slowly and may spoil. Or, if the temperature is too high, the food will cook or will harden on the outside but remain moist underneath, leading to deterioration or spoilage inside.

Which drying method is best?

There are over a half-dozen different ways to dry fruits and vegetables. Some produce excellent results; others don't. Here we will discuss three methods: drying in the sun, in a dehydrator, and in a conventional oven. (For drying in a convection oven, see page 121.) We'll consider the advantages and disadvantages of different methods and suggest which works best for a particular type of food.

When choosing a method, consider the quantity and quality of the food you plan to dry, as well as the time and money you wish to invest.

Sun drying is without doubt the oldest known method for preserving food. Fruits and vegetables just naturally shrivel and dry when exposed to the sun. Nature's simple process is essentially the way fruit drying is still done—the majority of commercially dried fruit, such as apricots, peaches, raisins, and figs, are dried by the sun.

Beside being the least expensive way to dehydrate food, sun drying can accommodate large quantities at one time. It does require a fair amount of time and effort, though. The most important requirement for sun drying is a number of days that reach a high temperature with a moderate to low humidity. The ideal locale would be an area that receives many consecutive hot days (85°F or higher) with relatively low humidity.

Oven drying, placing food to dry in an oven at temperatures between 130° to 150°F, is another way to dry food without going to much added expense. Unlike sun drying, which depends on the weather, oven drying can be done at any time of the day or night, rain or shine.

Unfortunately, many older ovens offer a minimum temperature of 200°F—too high for drying fruits and vegetables (though some meats can be dried at this temperature). Some modern ovens, including convection ovens, offer temperatures beginning as low as 125°F—more than low enough, since most foods are dried between 130° and 150°F.

While faster than sun drying, oven drying may take longer than drying in a dehydrator. Also, you must avoid oven drying foods that require sulfuring, since the fumes from sulfur dioxide are extremely irritating and may discolor inside of oven.

Drying in a dehydrator often produces the best quality product. A dehydrator is a box-shaped or circular appliance resembling a countertop oven (though some are larger). It maintains a low, even temperature and circulates the heated air by means of a blower or fan. Fruits, vegetables, and meats can be dried with little attention on your part at any time of the day or night. Larger units with many shelves allow you to dry much more food than you can handle in an oven. Some models, especially those without fans, require the trays be rearranged during the drying cycle.

A number of appliance manufacturers now offer some type of electric food dehydrator in their product lines. Most come equipped with a thermostat and several drying trays.

If you decide a dehydrator is worth the initial investment to you, consider these questions as you shop: How well is it constructed? Are the walls insulated and easy to clean? Do the drying trays slide out easily and accommodate ample quantities of food? Are additional trays avail-

Commercial dehydrator circulates constant, low, even heat

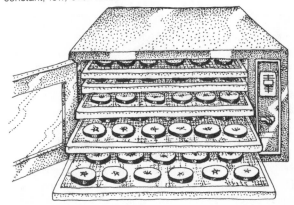

able? Does it have a thermostat? Are you satisfied with the manufacturer's warranty?

For procedures for drying in a dehydrator, consult the manufacturer's instructions.

DRYING FRESH FRUITS

First, read "Which drying method is best?" on page 101. Remember to choose the fruit varieties that give the best results. You'll find them listed in our "Guide for Drying Fruit" on page 108.

Always select fully ripe fruit in top condition. Larger fruits need to be sliced or cut. Some fruits benefit from a pretreatment using sulfur (see "Step-by-step directions for sulfuring,") sodium metabisulfite, or an antidarkening agent, page 104.

Have on hand all the equipment you'll need to finish the processing. After dried fruit has cooled to room temperature, loosely package in plastic bags, rigid plastic containers, or glass jars to "condition." Then pack in airtight containers for longer storage.

If the completely dried fruit is firmer than you'd like, try "tenderizing" it before eating by immersing it in boiling water for about 15 seconds. Drain well, then let dry on paper towels.

Why do some fruits discolor?

Some dark-colored fruits, such as figs, prunes, and grapes, dry nicely on their own when left exposed to the sun and wind. But fruits like apples, pears, apricots, and peaches turn brown when exposed to air. This chemical reaction, called *oxidation,* also robs the fruit of flavor and vitamins C and A.

In order to dry these light-colored fruits so they taste and look as good as commercially dried fruits, you must halt the oxidation process. The most effective method known today is to expose the cut fruit to the fumes of burning sulfur.

Other, less effective methods involve pretreating the fruit with sodium metabisulfite or with an anti-darkening agent such as lemon juice, ascorbic acid, or commercial powdered fruit preservative.

Sulfuring is the technique commercial fruit dryers use and is the one we recommend for home fruit drying because the fruit remains pliable and retains most of its original shape, color, and vitamins C and A. Sulfur prevents browning and also helps repel insects, speeds drying time, and inhibits mold growth. If properly done, sulfuring is perfectly safe and leaves no harmful residue on the fruit. You must, however, perform the sulfuring out-of-doors. Also, sulfured fruit must be dried out-of-doors, either in the sun or in a dehydrator placed outside.

Directions for sulfuring fruit appear on page 104. A chart on page 108 tells you for which fruits it is preferred, as well as the amount of sulfur to use.

Sulfiting is pretreating fruit by soaking it in a solution of water and sodium metabisulfite or bisulfite. Though it can be done safely inside, and though sulfited fruit can be dried either in the sun or in an oven or dehydrator, this method is not as effective as sulfuring; also, it increases the drying time required and yields a product of poorer quality.

If you do choose sulfiting, you can purchase sodium metabisulfite or sulfur bisulfite (either type is fine) from a drugstore, a winemaking supply store, or some chemical companies in large quantities.

Mix 2 teaspoons sodium metabisulfite with 1 quart of water in a large bowl and add the cut fruit to the solution. It's important not to leave cut fruit in this soaking solution too long (it may become mushy). Most slices of fruit should be left in for 10 minutes; halved fruit can remain up to 30 minutes.

After soaking, remove fruit, drain, then place on drying trays. Sun drying times for sulfited fruit are 15 to 20 percent longer than for sulfured fruit.

(Continued on page 104)

If they're going to nibble between meals anyway, at least you can tempt them to nibble nutritiously. Here are wholesome treats for the trail or the after-school kitchen raid—clockwise from top are apricot, raspberry, strawberry, and plum fruit leathers (page 112); dried banana chips (chart, page 121); fruit & seed bars (page 107); dried apple rings (chart, page 108); dried fruit trail mix (page 105); and dried fruit newtons (page 107). At top right are walnuts in shells.

Antidarkening agents such as ascorbic acid, as well as sodium metabisulfite, may be used to help prevent browning during preparation for a short time. While these methods are not considered pretreatments like sulfuring and sulfiting (see page 102), they are useful in postponing dis-coloration while you finish cutting up fruit.

Soak cut fruit in solution of sodium metabisulfite (or bisulfite) and water

In a large bowl, mix 1 tablespoon ascorbic acid OR ¼ teaspoon sodium metabisulfite with a quart of water. Cut fruit directly into the bowl; the fruit can stand in the holding solution for up to an hour. Drain the fruit well and dry it.

You can also use a commercial powdered fruit preservative—a mixture of L-ascorbate, sugar and sometimes citric acid—following package directions.

Step-by-step directions for sulfuring fruit

Sulfuring prevents cut fruit from discoloring by retarding oxidation. Always done outdoors, it requires that the fruit be arranged on wooden trays that, when stacked and placed under cover, allow fumes of burning sulfur to circulate freely. Once fruit has been sulfured, it may be dried in the sun or in a dehydrator that's been placed outdoors. *Never dry sulfured fruit indoors* in a dehydrator or in a conventional or convection oven—fumes are harmful when inhaled.

1 With few alterations, wood fruit-packing lugs or crates (about 17½ by 13½ inches) make ideal trays for sulfuring fruit and for drying, as well. Look for lugs at the supermarket or at your local fruit stand.

2 You'll need a large cardboard box, such as the packing cartons large appliances come in—an oven or range carton covers five or six trays, and a refrigerator or freezer carton covers up to 10 trays. Make sure the box is free of large cracks or holes (small ones can be covered with masking tape). Cut a flap in the box near the bottom so you can reach inside to light the sulfur; cut a similar hole in the top (see illustration below).

3 You'll also need two concrete building blocks (each about 8 by 8 by 16 inches), an 8-inch foil pie pan, and flowers of sulfur (also called "sublimed sulfur"), which may be purchased at nurseries and garden supply centers. Check the label to see that the sulfur is at least 99.8 percent pure.

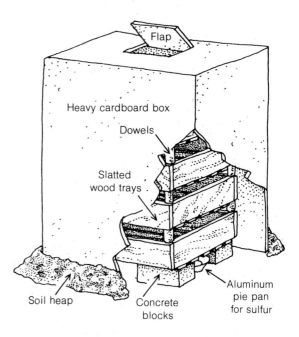

Flap

Heavy cardboard box

Dowels

Slatted wood trays

Soil heap

Concrete blocks

Aluminum pie pan for sulfur

4 Select an outdoor spot of dirt or gravel, away from planted areas. Dig a shallow pit to hold the foil pan of sulfur. Place concrete blocks on either side of pit.

5 Weigh the fruit you plan to sulfur; then calculate the amount of sulfur you'll need, following the chart on page 108. Place sulfur in pan; set pan in pit between blocks.

6 Line each drying tray with a double layer of cheesecloth; arrange prepared fruit in a single layer, cut side up, on cloth, spreading pieces apart slightly.

7 Carefully balance drying tray on blocks, centered over foil pan below. Stack remaining trays, one on top of the other.

8 Cover all with cardboard box—arrange it so it clears the trays by at least 1½ inches on all sides. Push dirt against bottom edges of box to seal.

9 Open the two flaps you cut in box. Reach through bottom hole and light sulfur with a match. After 5 minutes, peek through bottom hole to check that sulfur is burning.

10 When the sulfur has burned for about 5 minutes longer, close both flaps. You may want to secure flaps closed with masking tape.

11 Sulfuring times vary with the type of fruit, the size of the pieces, and the kind of equipment used. Most fruit requires from 1 to 4 hours of exposure to the fumes of burning sulfur. Even though the burning may appear to be over, the sulfur dioxide fumes trapped in the box are still working. Fruit can be left for 12 to 14 hours in the sulfuring box if desired. *Be careful not to inhale the sulfur dioxide fumes*—they can be harmful to your lungs and irritating to mucous membranes.

12 After sulfuring is completed, remove box and arrange trays in the sun, following directions for sun drying below. Or place fruit in a dehydrator (make sure it is located outside in a well-ventilated area) and dry, following manufacturer's instructions.

Step-by-step directions for sun drying fruit

1 Select fruit that is fully ripe but not mushy—fruit that is in top condition for eating fresh. Sort and wash, discarding any pieces that show signs of spoilage (unless spoiled part can be cut away). Prepare individual fruits as directed on chart on page 108. If you're drying light-colored fruits, read "Why do some fruits discolor?" on page 102, and pretreat as needed.

2 Line each drying tray with a double layer of cheesecloth. (Trays can be stackable trays used for sulfuring, clean shallow cardboard or wooden boxes with holes or slits, screen stretched over wooden frames, or rimmed baking pans.) Spread pieces slightly apart on cheesecloth.

3 Arrange trays in direct sun, off the ground, on benches or a table, if possible. To protect from insects, cover trays with a single layer of cheesecloth or nylon netting, stretching it taut so it doesn't touch fruit. Secure edges with tape or string.

4 Check fruit frequently, moving trays when they become shaded. If you live where nights are relatively clear and temperatures don't drop more than about 20° F below midday highs, you can leave stacked, covered trays of fruit outdoors. Otherwise, take trays to a porch or other place at night.

Fruit dried in baking pans or trays without holes must be turned over after the juice in pit cavity has dried and then again each day until dry.

If it's necessary to take fruit indoors for any length of time (if it rains!), lift cover occasionally and check to see if any mold is forming. If mold does form, moisten a cloth with white vinegar or with a solution of 1 tablespoon household liquid bleach (sodium hypochlorite) to 1 quart water and wipe off mold.

5 Cool a piece of fruit and test for doneness, using guidelines found in chart on page 108. When done, take fruit indoors and let it cool completely.

6 Loosely pack dried fruit in plastic bags, rigid plastic containers, or glass jars; close containers and store at room temperature for 5 to 7 days. This "mellowing time" allows excess moisture in some pieces to be absorbed by the drier ones. Occasionally, shake bags to separate pieces.

7 Package fruit, following instructions under "Packaging & storing dried food," page 116.

Dried Fruit Recipes

Dried Fruit Trail Mix
(Pictured on page 103)

This nutritious trail mix combines the exotic flavors of dried banana chips, papaya slices, and pitted dates. You'll find all of these dried fruits at most health food stores.

(Continued on page 107)

½ cup *each* dried papaya slices, un-sweetened shredded coconut, and dried banana chips
¼ cup *each* dark and golden raisins
⅓ cup chopped pitted dates
¼ cup chopped dried apricots

Cut papaya and break banana chips into bite-size pieces. Place in a large bowl along with other ingredients. Toss gently until well blended. Package in airtight containers or plastic bags. Store in a cool place for up to 2 weeks. Makes about 3 cups.

Fruit & Seed Bars
(Pictured on page 103)

In these nutritious bars, seeds, nuts, and dried fruit are held together by a light coating of honey and brown sugar. You can use any dried fruit, such as dates, raisins, apples, or apricots.

1 cup sesame seeds
½ cup *each* chopped nuts (unsalted peanuts, cashews, or almonds) and sunflower seeds or pumpkin seeds
½ cup *each* firmly packed brown sugar and honey
¼ teaspoon salt
½ cup *each* dried fruit (see suggestions above) and unsweetened shredded coconut
Butter

Combine sesame seeds, chopped nuts, and sunflower or pumpkin seeds. Spread in a thin layer on a rimmed baking sheet. Roast in a 350°F oven for about 15 minutes or until light golden, shaking pan occasionally; set aside.

In a wide frying pan over medium heat, combine brown sugar, honey, salt and dried fruit. Bring mixture to a boil, stirring constantly, and cook for 2 minutes. Remove pan from heat and immediately stir in seeds, nuts, and coconut; mix thoroughly. Turn into a well-buttered, shallow 9 by 13-inch baking dish. With a large, buttered spoon, press mixture firmly and evenly over bottom.

Let cool at room temperature for 30 minutes, then lift out with a wide spatula. Use a large

knife to cut into 1½ by 3-inch rectangles. When no longer sticky (after about 3 hours), wrap individual pieces or several pieces together in plastic wrap. Store at room temperature. Makes 22 bars.

Dried Fruit Cordials
(Pictured on facing page)

Dried apricots, peaches, pears, and prunes—immersed even briefly in fortified white wine—will give the wine a delightful natural fruitiness. These cordials grow smoother the longer they stand, and they make imaginative gifts from your kitchen.

Light and fresh, the liqueurs are excellent for sipping and delicious as a topping on ice cream or fresh fruit. Even the dried fruits themselves take on new character—the apricots and prunes are particularly delicious.

The combination of dry white wine, brandy, and sugar gives the cordials longevity and delicacy. Because the fruit rapidly mellows any harshness, you can use inexpensive wine and brandy.

1 pound dried fruit (apricots, prunes with pits, pears, or peaches)
1 bottle (4/5 quart) or 3½ cups dry white wine
1 cup brandy
2 cups sugar

Place dried fruit in a glass, ceramic, or stainless steel container. Stir in wine, brandy, and sugar until well blended. Cover tightly. Let stand at room temperature for at least 1 week to allow flavors to develop, stirring occasionally for the first few days until sugar is dissolved.

After 1 week apricots, prunes, and pears should be soft; peaches should be still slightly firm. Fruit flavor of wine reaches maximum intensity in 3 or 4 weeks. After about 6 weeks, if fruit becomes too soft, remove it; wine keeps indefinitely.

To serve, offer a piece of fruit with a glass of wine or serve them separately. To give these fruit cordials as gifts, repack in small containers with tight-fitting lids. Makes about 1½ quarts.

Dried Fruit Newtons
(Pictured on page 103)

Our recipe for homemade newtons calls for wheat germ and whole wheat flour; you can choose from dried figs, prunes, apricots, or dates for the filling. The cookies will look best if you roll out the dough carefully so it has straight edges.

(Continued on next page)

Mellow-sweet and beautiful, fruit cordials make elegant after-dinner drinks served here with cocoa-covered almonds. Choices (left to right) are peach, pear, and apricot. The recipe is on this page.

1 **cup whole wheat flour, unsifted**

1¼ **cups all-purpose flour, unsifted**

¼ **cup wheat germ**

¼ **teaspoon *each* salt and baking soda**

½ **cup (¼ lb.) butter or margarine, softened**

½ **cup *each* granulated and firmly packed brown sugar**

2 **eggs**

½ **teaspoon vanilla**

Choice of dried-fruit filling (recipes on page 109)

Combine whole wheat and all-purpose flours, wheat germ, salt, and baking soda. In a large bowl, beat butter until creamy; gradually beat in granulated and brown sugars until fluffy. Beat in eggs and vanilla. Stir in flour mixture until blended. Knead dough lightly until smooth. Cover and refrigerate for at least 1 hour or until next day. Prepare filling; refrigerate.

Divide dough, returning half to refrigerator. On a floured board, roll out remaining dough to a clean-edged 9 by 15-inch rectangle; cut into 3 strips, each 3 by 15 inches. Repeat with chilled dough.

Divide filling into 6 equal portions and spread 1 portion down center of each strip, bringing it evenly out to edges. Use a long spatula to lift sides of each dough strip over filling, overlapping slightly on top. Press edges together lightly. Cut strips in half; lift and invert, seam side down, onto a greased baking sheet. Brush off excess flour. Refrigerate for about 15 minutes.

Bake in a 375°F oven for 15 to 20 minutes or until lightly browned. Partially cool on wire racks. Cut each strip into 4 pieces. Cool completely and store, covered, at room temperature for up to a week; freeze for longer storage. (The cookies will be softer and more flavorful after they've stood at least a day.) Makes 4 dozen.

(Continued on next page)

Guide for Drying Fruit

Fruit	How to prepare	Treatment before drying	Test for dryness (Cool a piece before testing)
Apples Firm varieties: Gravenstein, Yellow Newtown Pippin, Rome Beauty, Jonathan	Peel, cut off both ends. Either cut out core and slice apples into ¼"-thick rings, or cut into ¼"-thick slices, removing core.	Sulfuring is preferred. Use 2 teaspoons sulfur per pound of cut fruit.	Soft, leathery, pliable
Apricots Blenheim (Royal), Tilton	Wash, cut in half, remove pits.	Sulfuring is preferred. Use 1 teaspoon per pound of cut fruit.	Soft, pliable, slightly moist in center when cut
Figs Black Mission, Kadota	(Leave figs on tree; when fully ripe and ready for drying, they fall to the ground.) Wash; cut in half or leave whole.	No treatment necessary.	Leathery outside but still pliable. Slightly sticky inside, but not wet
Grapes Thompson Seedless, Muscat	Wash, leave whole. Leave stems on until after fruit is dried.	No treatment necessary.	Raisinlike texture, wrinkled
Nectarines and **Peaches** Freestone varieties	Wash, cut in half, remove pits. Peeling not necessary but will result in better-looking dried fruit.	Sulfuring is preferred. Use 2 teaspoons sulfur per pound of cut fruit.	Soft, pliable, slightly moist in center when cut
Pears Bartlett	Wash, peel, cut in half, core.	Sulfuring is preferred. Use 2½ teaspoons sulfur per pound of cut fruit.	Soft, pliable, slightly moist in center when cut
Prunes French, Standard, and Italian	Wash, cut in half, remove pits.	No treatment necessary.	Flesh firm but still pliable

Dried-fig filling. Using a food processor or food chopper, grind 1 pound **dried figs** (about 2 cups) and ½ cup **walnuts** or almonds. Turn into a pan and stir in ⅓ cup **sugar**, ½ cup **water**, 1 teaspoon **grated lemon peel**, and 2 tablespoons **lemon juice.** Cook over medium heat, stirring, for 5 to 8 minutes or until boiling and thickened. Let cool.

Prune filling. Substitute 2 cups pitted **prunes** for figs in above recipe. Add ¾ teaspoon **ground cinnamon** with sugar.

Apricot filling. Substitute 3 cups **dried apricots** for figs and 1 teaspoon **grated orange peel** for lemon peel in above recipe.

Date filling. Substitute 1 pound pitted **dates** for figs in above recipe and increase **lemon peel** to 2 teaspoons.

Dried Fruit Compote

From Lebanon comes an interesting recipe using dried fruit and nuts to make a tempting compote. You'll need about 3 cups of dried fruit such as apricots, raisins, pitted prunes, figs or packaged mixed dried fruit. Suggestions for combining fruits follow.

- ⅔ cup sugar (or ½ cup honey)
- 4½ cups water
- 3 cups dried fruit (directions follow)
- ⅓ cup *each* halved blanched almonds and pine nuts (or ⅔ cup almonds)
- 1 teaspoon *each* orange-flower water and rose water (or 1 cinnamon stick and 3 whole allspice)
- ½ cup pomegranate seeds (optional)
  Chopped walnuts
  Whipped cream

In a 3-quart pan, combine sugar and water. Bring to simmering over medium heat, stirring

until sugar dissolves; reduce heat and simmer gently, uncovered, for 5 minutes.

Meanwhile, assemble mixed fruit. Some good combinations are: 1 cup *each* apricots, raisins, and prunes or figs; 1½ cups apricots and ¾ cup *each* prunes and raisins; or 1 package (12 oz.) mixed dried fruit (remove prune pits) and ½ cup raisins. Cut large fruit into bite-size pieces.

Mix the fruit into the syrup and add almonds and pine nuts. Stir in orange-flower water and rose water. Cover and simmer until fruits are tender, about 8 to 12 minutes.

Let cool to lukewarm; remove spices (if used) and add pomegranate seeds, if desired. Spoon into individual dishes; chill well. Serve topped with chopped walnuts and a dollop of whipped cream. Makes about 6 servings.

High-Energy Trail Logs

Backpackers will applaud these hearty little nuggets of energy. They can be served at home as snacks, too. Seal them in plastic wrap; they'll keep in the refrigerator for several weeks.

- ¼ cup dry-roasted cashews
- 1¼ cups walnuts
- 6 dried black figs
- ½ cup pitted dates
- ½ cup golden seedless raisins
- ¼ cup dried apples
- ½ teaspoon lemon juice
- 1 tablespoon dark or light rum
- 2 tablespoons powdered sugar or about ½ cup flaked coconut

Using a food processor or a food chopper with fine blade, grind nuts and fruits and mix thoroughly. Blend in lemon juice and rum. Using about a tablespoon at a time, roll the mixture into small logs, each about ¾ by 2 inches. Roll the logs in powdered sugar or coconut and allow to stand uncovered for one or two days to dry. Store in refrigerator or wrap individually in foil or plastic wrap to carry on the trail. Makes about 2½ dozen.

Scandinavian Dried Fruit Soup

Chunks of fresh pineapple combine with orange juice and sun-dried fruits to make this refreshing Scandinavian-style soup. For dried fruit, choose several kinds—apples, apricots, figs, peaches, pears, or pitted prunes—to make 2½ cups.

(Continued on next page)

2½ cups mixed dried fruit (suggestions above), cut into bite-size pieces

½ cup raisins

1 stick cinnamon

½ lemon, thinly sliced

3½ cups water

2 cups orange juice

1½ cups fresh or canned unsweetened pineapple chunks (drained)

⅔ to ¾ cup honey (to taste)

⅛ teaspoon salt

2 tablespoons quick-cooking tapioca

⅓ cup rum or brandy

Vanilla yogurt or sour cream

In a 3-quart pan, combine dried fruit, raisins, cinnamon, lemon slices, water and orange juice; bring to a boil over high heat. Reduce heat to medium low, cover, and simmer for 10 minutes.

Remove from heat and add pineapple, honey, salt, tapioca, and rum. Let stand for 5 minutes to allow tapioca to soften.

Return mixture to medium-low heat and cook, uncovered, for 12 to 15 minutes or until mixture thickens and fruit is tender but not mushy. Serve hot, or cover and refrigerate to serve cold. Top with spoonfuls of yogurt or sour cream. Makes 6 to 8 servings.

Chewy Apricot-Bran Cookies

These cookies are packed with wholesome cereals, nuts, and dried fruits. They offer quick, easily handled nourishment to start the day—a boon to late risers and those who prefer a lighter approach to the morning meal.

⅓ cup whole bran cereal (not bran flakes)

¼ cup water

¾ cup butter or margarine, softened

½ cup firmly packed brown sugar

1 egg

¼ cup honey

1 teaspoon vanilla

1 cup all-purpose flour

1 teaspoon *each* soda and salt

¼ cup dry milk

1 cup *each* regular rolled oats and finely chopped dried apricots

¾ cup chopped walnuts

Combine bran and water in a small bowl; set aside.

In a large bowl, beat together butter and brown sugar until creamy. Add egg and beat until fluffy. Mix in honey, vanilla, and bran.

Combine flour, soda, salt, dry milk, oats, apricots, and walnuts. Stir into creamed mixture. Drop by level tablespoonfuls onto greased cooky sheets, placing dough about 2 inches apart.

Bake in a 375° oven for 10 minutes or until golden brown and firm when lightly touched. Makes about 3 dozen cookies.

Wholesome Fruit & Bran Muffins

Few foods are as accommodating as muffins—you can load them with nutritious ingredients and they taste better for it. Because they're so full of fruit and other moist ingredients, they keep well in the refrigerator or freezer. Serve them hot, cold, or reheated.

1½ cups whole bran cereal (not bran flakes)

½ cup boiling water

1 egg, lightly beaten

1 cup buttermilk

½ cup honey

¼ cup melted butter or margarine

1½ cups mixed dried fruit (raisins, chopped dates, prunes, or figs)

½ cup *each* chopped nuts and whole wheat flour, unsifted

¾ cup all-purpose flour, unsifted

½ teaspoon salt

1¼ teaspoons soda

In a large bowl, combine bran cereal with water; stir to moisten evenly, then allow to cool until lukewarm. Stir in egg, buttermilk, honey, butter, dried fruit, and nuts until well blended.

In another bowl, combine whole wheat and all-purpose flours, salt, and soda. Combine dry ingredients with liquid ingredients; stir just until evenly moistened. Spoon into greased or paper-lined muffin pans, filling them ¾ full. Bake in a 425° oven for 20 to 25 minutes or until pick inserted in center comes out clean. Makes 12 to 16 muffins.

Bedecked with dill sprigs, in Scandinavian fashion, smoke-cooked salmon fillet provides a sumptuous first course with cucumber slices and parsley-dappled new potatoes. The recipe appears on page 122.

FRUIT LEATHERS

(Pictured on page 103)

It's a cloudless morning with sunny weather promising to hold for several more days. You have a good supply of ripe fruit or perhaps some succulent but imperfect leftovers from canning or making preserves. It's an ideal opportunity to make fruit leathers.

This age-old process couldn't be simpler. The lightly sweetened purées of fruits and berries, spread in thin layers and left in the sun, dry into translucent sheets of fruit that are chewy and flavorful.

Rolled sheets of these dried fruits, similar to our homemade ones, have been sold in food markets for several years and are now quite widely available. Here's how you can make your own fruit leathers.

Setting up

Start early in the day. You'll need a smooth level surface, such as a table; a place to put it in full sun; and a roll of plastic wrap, plus tape, cheesecloth, and two boards. Tear off strips of plastic wrap, stretch it across the drying surface, and fasten with tape. To keep the fruit clean while drying, stretch a sheet of cheesecloth over it; you can secure it to two 2 by 4-inch boards on either side, taking care to keep it from touching the purée.

Preparing fruit

Fruit should be fully ripe. Wash and prepare each as directed below. Cut away any blemishes; then measure (up to 5 pints for any one batch). Add sugar and heat as directed for each fruit. Remove from heat and whirl (part at a time, if necessary) in a blender or food processor, or put through a food mill or wire strainer; cool to lukewarm. Pour purée onto prepared surface and spread to ¼ inch thick (a full 5-pint batch covers a 30-inch-long strip of 12-inch-wide plastic wrap.)

Apricots. Remove pits and measure halves; use 1½ tablespoons sugar for each cup fruit. Crush while heating to just below boiling (about 180°F).

Berries. Remove stems and measure whole berries; use 1 tablespoon sugar for each cup strawberries, 1½ tablespoons sugar for each cup raspberries, or 2½ tablespoons sugar for each cup blackberries. Bring strawberries just to full rolling boil. Boil other berries, stirring, until liquid appears syrupy; then put through a food mill or wire strainer to remove some of the seeds; spread berry mixture about 3/16 inch thick.

Peaches and nectarines. Choose yellow freestone peaches, such as Rio Oso, Redhaven, Elberta; peel peaches (do not peel nectarines); slice and measure. Use 1½ tablespoons sugar for each cup fruit. Crush while heating to just below boiling, about 180°F. (If liquid is thin, boil until it appears syrupy.)

Plums. Choose varieties with firm flesh, such as Santa Rosa, Mariposa, Nubiana; slice and measure. Use 2½ tablespoons sugar for each cup Santa Rosa, about 1½ tablespoons sugar for each cup other plums. Crush while heating to just below boiling, about 180°F. (If liquid is thin, boil until it appears syrupy.)

The drying

It may take 20 to 24 hours for leather to dry, depending on the fruit and the sun's heat. By the end of the first day it should be dry enough that you can loosen tape, slip a baking sheet underneath, and carry it inside; return to sun the next morning.

When firm to touch, try peeling the fruit sheet off the plastic. It is sufficiently dry when the whole sheet can be pulled off the plastic with no purée adhering. (Don't leave in sun longer than needed.) In humid climates, you may need to finish the drying indoors. Set the sheets of fruit on pans in a 140° to 150°F oven and leave oven door slightly open.

For storing. Roll up sheets of fruit leather while on plastic wrap, then wrap that with more plastic and seal tightly. Color and flavor keep well about one month at room temperature, four months in refrigerator, or one year if frozen.

DRYING VEGETABLES

Drying vegetables involves slightly different procedures from drying fruit—the difference here is that you blanch the vegetables before drying. Like fruit, if vegetables aren't in prime condition, they won't be good for drying. Though they can be sun dried, better ways of drying are to use your oven, or a dehydrator oven (see page 101).

For oven drying, you'll need drying trays, an accurate thermometer, and a small fan. For drying vegetables in a dehydrator, follow manufacturer's instructions.

For sun drying, you'll need a temperature of 100°F (higher than for fruit) and relatively low humidity. If one or the other is unreliable, spoilage will probably occur before the vegetables can completely dry. It will take about 3 to 4 days for this process, and vegetables need to be chopped into small sizes no larger than ½-inch cubes. You must remember to bring the trays of vegetables into the house at night if the temperature outside drops 20° F between day and night.

The chart on pages 117–118 will give you preparation steps required for each vegetable, as well as the best varieties to use, blanching methods and times, and tests to determine dryness.

First, you blanch

Blanching is the process of heating vegetables sufficiently to inactivate enzymes. If the enzymes are not inactivated, deterioration will result during drying and storage. Unblanched vegetables (except for chili peppers, onions, celery, and garlic) will have poorer flavor and color after they have been dried. Blanching may be done in hot water or in steam.

Water blanching. Use only enough water to cover the vegetables. Bring water to a boil and gradually stir in the vegetables, following directions on the chart for each vegetable. Reuse the same water for blanching additional batches of the same vegetable, adding new water as necessary. Keep a lid on the container when blanching. Cool immediately by plunging under cold running water.

Steam blanching. You'll need a pot with a tight-fitting lid to use as a steaming container, and a colander, wire basket, or sieve that will fit into the steaming container.

Add 1½ to 2 inches water to the pot and heat to boiling. Place the colander, loosely packed with vegetables, into the pot, cover, and leave until they are heated through and wilted. Check the chart for blanching times. Test by cutting through the center of a vegetable to see if it looks cooked (translucent) almost to the center.

Step-by-step directions for oven drying vegetables

1 Load two to four oven drying trays (see page 101) with 4 to 6 pounds of prepared vegetables (trimmed weight). Distribute vegetables evenly between the trays in a single layer. Don't dry odorous vegetables (cauliflower or broccoli) with any other vegetable.

2 Place a thermometer on the top tray toward the back of the oven.

3 Preheat oven to 140°–150°F and add loaded trays. Prop open the oven door at least 4 inches.

4 Place a small fan outside oven so air will circulate through the open door and across the oven. Change the fan's position from side to side during drying period.

(Continued on page 116)

Growing your own vegetables gives you the chance to enjoy them at their best. But figuring out exactly when they reach that plump, sweet stage is trickier than veteran vegetable growers often make it seem.

Harvesting too soon keeps the crops from reaching full size and, often, full flavor. *Harvesting too late* may increase size, but at the expense of flavor and tenderness. And a vegetable left on the plant too long drains energy and slows further production.

In August, when most crops grow rapidly, it's a good idea to check their progress every day. Hunt thoroughly for ripe or aging vegetables and pick right away. If you go away during harvest time, have someone come in to pick vegetables as they ripen.

In addition to the signs of ripeness given in the following list, there's a simple test that works for many vegetables: pick a few samples and taste for sweetness and crispness.

Asparagus. This perennial crop should grow undisturbed the first season after planting. During the second spring, cut spears for 4 to 6 weeks; then permit foliage to grow to strengthen the root system for next year's crop. In subsequent springs, cut for 8 to 10 weeks. Discontinue cutting when thin spears begin to appear; these show that root strength is declining.

Cut spears at ground level or 1½ inches below; don't cut deeply enough to injure root crown.

Use a sharp knife or (preferably) an asparagus knife with a V-shaped notch for a cutting edge.

Beans (green or wax). Look for young, tender, long, sleek pods with beans just starting to bulge sides. Simplest test is to taste a few for crispness and sweetness. Or test by breaking in half; at their best, beans will snap with a pop, show no or few fibers. Aging pods turn yellow, leathery, stringy, streaked; beans inside are mealy.

Beets. The smaller the better, once beety flavor develops; best when 1 to 2 inches in diameter. You can eat tops and roots of small beets you thin out. Old beets bump out of the ground, have split sides, taste woody. Pickle surplus rather than leave them in the ground. To harvest greens, cut when foliage is dark, before leaves turn yellow.

Broccoli. Cut while clustered flower heads are firm and green. Take heads with leaves and 5 or 6 inches of stem (also edible). Don't damage short side branches; they will produce smaller heads if left to grow.

Brussels sprouts. Twist or snap off sprouts when they are firm and still deep green (usually about the time lowest big leaves start to yellow). Harvest lowest sprouts first. Upper ones will continue to enlarge to harvesting size.

Cabbage. Harvest when heads are firm to the touch. Cut off head and a few wrapper leaves with a sharp knife.

Carrots. Young ones are sweetest and most tender; start pulling at finger size or when you need to thin crowded plants. Except for biggest varieties, carrots turn woody when over 1½ inches in diameter. In tight soil, water first; then carefully tug and tease carrots to avoid breaking them or injuring neighboring ones.

Cauliflower. As soon as blossom heads begin to form, tie up outer leaves over them to shade them from the sun. This is a blanching process and it produces a white head of cauliflower. Inspect from time to time and before the flower sections begin to separate.

Corn. Good timing is critical because sugar in kernels turns to starch as soon as ear is picked or reaches a certain age—and then it's no better than storebought. Perfectionists say to start the water boiling and then go out and pick.

As first sign of coming ripeness, green silks wither to brown; feel for plump kernels through husk. To make sure corn is ripe, peel back husk at top and pierce a kernel with thumbnail. Milky juice spurts out if ear is just right. Clear juice means wait a day or two. Insides like toothpaste mean you've missed your chance for perfection on that ear.

Cucumber. With most varieties, pick for sweet pickles when 2 to 3 inches long, for dills when 5 to 6 inches, for slicing when 6 to 8 inches. Lemon cucumber should measure no wider than 3 inches. Japanese and Armenian cucumbers retain quality even up to 20 inches long. Cut or snap off, leaving short stem.

Eggplant. It's most tender and you hardly notice small seeds if you pick when glossy, dark purple, and 4 to 6 inches long (it can grow much larger). Pick long, slender Japanese eggplant when finger size to hot-dog size; one plant will bear dozens if you keep them picked.

Lima beans. Pods should be green, with swellings to show the beans inside. Open a pod or two; beans should be plump but still green or gray green (not white). Pick often to prolong picking season.

Melons. These are tricky. Smell is as good a clue as any (except for watermelon); sniff for characteristic aroma at blossom end.

Cantaloupe. Nudge gently; if it slips from the stem, it's ready. Another sign: Netting on skin becomes prominent.

Casaba. Leave on the vine until blossom end softens and rind turns yellow.

Crenshaw. It's ripe (and highly perishable) when dark green skin turns yellow.

Honeydew. Pick when blossom end softens and white skin turns cream color.

Watermelon. Think about harvesting when curly tendril on vine next to fruit stem withers. Further confirmation: Where rind touches ground, it turns from white to light yellow. Folk method of rapping on melon works if you have a good ear: ripe melon goes "pong" instead of "ping."

Onions and garlic. You can use some onions green and leave the rest to grow up. Pull green onions when stalk is thick as a pencil; even young ones have good flavor. Harvest dry onions

and garlic when tops dry up and fall over. (You can harvest sooner, but bulbs won't store well.) Loosen ground with spade or fork, then tug them out. Let bulbs dry on top of ground for a few days. Remove tops before storing.

Parsnips. Use as soon as roots are large enough to cook. Or, if you wish, leave roots in ground until needed. They will tolerate almost any cold, but of course you can't dig them if the ground is frozen solid. Use before spring regrowth.

Peas. A simple test is to pick and taste a few. Peas inside the pods should be tender and deep green. Pick frequently to prolong production.

Some edible pod peas—sugar or snow peas—should be picked as soon as peas are perceptible inside the pods. Snap peas can be picked at that point or can be allowed to mature—but pick while peas inside are still green and plump.

Peppers. Pick sweet green peppers (bell peppers) any time after they reach worthwhile size. If left to mature, late in the season they turn bright red, mellow, and sweet. Pick hot peppers when they have reached full size and desired color—red, yellow, or green.

Potatoes. Start digging new potatoes when plants bloom; use right away or keep in refrigerator. Harvest old potatoes when tops die back; slip spade or fork deep under clump and lift to surface. Leave in sun only long enough for soil to dry; shake off soil. Store in cool, dark, dry place.

Spinach. Cut or pinch off outer leaves to eat as they reach full size. Let small inner ones grow to prolong harvest.

Squash. Zucchini and other long green summer squashes

are most tender between 5 and 8 inches long (up to 10 inches for some varieties). At ultimate size of 2 feet and more, they become fibrous, seedy, and tough skinned. Bake overgrown squash if skin is still tender enough for you to pierce it with light push of thumbnail. Blooms can turn into edible-size squash in a couple of nights; search plants every other day.

Yellow crookneck varieties taste best when 4 to 7 inches long. Pick when pale yellow rather than golden, before skin hardens.

Scalloped squash (pattypan) should be harvested when it's grayish or greenish white, before it turns ivory white. It's best while small, even silver-dollar size.

Winter squash (acorn, Hubbard, spaghetti) and *pumpkins* develop hard shells and can be stored until spring if allowed to mature. Pick after vine dries up. Leave on the ground until frost, if you want, but in hot valleys harvest or protect from sunburn when vine foliage withers away. Cut with 2 or 3-inch stems on. Store in dry place between 45° and 55°F.

Tomatoes. Wait for deep red color (except for yellow and orange varieties) and firm flesh. To beat frosts at end of season, pick all fruit on vine and let green ones ripen in a warm place.

Turnips and rutabagas. Pull young plants with tiny roots to thin rows and give growing room to the remaining plants. Eat thinnings, tops and all. At 2-inch diameters, roots are tastiest, and tops are still good as greens. At 3 inches and above, roots are still good and store a little better. Late-planted rutabagas can stay in the ground until needed.

5 Maintain oven temperature at 140°F. It takes less heat to keep this temperature toward end of the drying period. (Reduce temperature to about 130°F toward end to prevent scorching.)

6 Check vegetables often and turn trays frequently to prevent scorching, especially at end of period.

7 Cool a piece of vegetable and test for doneness, using guidelines found in chart on page 117. Time required for drying varies (from 6 to 16 hours) depending on type of vegetable, size of pieces, and load on tray.

Packaging & storing dried food

Dried fruits and vegetables should be packaged as soon as possible after completely cooling.

Sun dried fruits often benefit from a 5 to 7-day mellowing or conditioning time to redistribute excess moisture from some pieces of fruit to others. To condition, loosely pack fruit in plastic bags, rigid plastic containers, or glass jars; cover tightly and let stand at room temperature for 5 to 7 days. (Shake containers occasionally to prevent sticking.) Vegetables needn't be conditioned in this manner, since most excess moisture is removed during drying.

If fruits or vegetables have been exposed to insects before or during the drying process, it is necessary to treat the food to prevent ingestion later on. The easiest way is to seal thoroughly dried food in heavy plastic bags, then place in the freezer for at least 48 hours (or up to 2 weeks). This kills any insects or their eggs that might be present.

To store dried fruit, seal in heavy plastic bags or rigid plastic containers

To package fruit and vegetables for long-term storage, pack into containers as tightly as possible without crushing. Heavy plastic bags are excellent because almost all the excess air can be squeezed out—better still are heat sealing plastic bags that lock out all air; however, glass jars or other airtight containers with tight-fitting lids may be used.

Store containers in a dry, cool, dark place. The coolest spot in the house may be the basement. Remember that for all dried foods, the cooler the storage spot, the longer the shelf life. If you're unable to find a storage place that is dark, wrap all clear containers with paper or foil, since light will fade food colors.

The length of time dried food can be satisfactorily stored obviously varies with the type of food, the conditions for drying, and the location of storage. However, a general rule would be to keep fruit and vegetables from 6 to 12 months. Dried fruit stored in the freezer keeps up to 2 years.

To ensure the best quality of home-dried foods, remember these points:

• Package dried food in moisture-resistant, airtight containers such as heavy plastic bags, glass jars, or rigid plastic containers with tight-fitting lids.

• Control fluctuations in temperature, humidity, and light. A cool, dark, dry location is best.

• Label and use dried foods as you would canned goods, placing packages of newly prepared ones to the rear, thus eliminating any doubt as to which ones have been stored the longest.

Rehydrating & cooking dried vegetables

Dried vegetables are not as easily prepared as fresh, frozen, or canned ones. They must be rehydrated—the removed water must be added back—by either soaking or cooking, or both.

To rehydrate vegetables before cooking, soak them in liquid such as broth or water. Though different vegetables absorb different amounts of liquid, we recommend covering 1 cup dried vegetables with 1½ cups boiling water or broth and letting them stand for 20 to 30 minutes, stirring occasionally, until vegetables have absorbed most of the liquid. If they absorb the liquid quickly but still look shriveled, add about ½ cup more boiling liquid and let stand until the shriveled look is reduced. Cook rehydrated vegetables as you would fresh ones.

Guide for Drying Vegetables

Vegetable	Best for drying	How to prepare	Test for dryness (Cool a piece before testing)
Artichokes	Use only tender hearts	Cut hearts into ⅛" strips. *To blanch,* heat in boiling solution of ¾ cup water and 1 tablespoon lemon juice for 6–8 minutes, depending on size.	Brittle
Asparagus	Use only tender tips	Wash thoroughly and halve large tips. *Blanch* (as directed on page 113), with steam 4–5 minutes or in water 3½–4½ minutes.	Leathery to brittle
Beans	Use only tender stringless varieties	Wash thoroughly. Cut in short pieces or lengthwise. *Blanch* (as directed on page 113), with steam for 3½–4 minutes or in water 3 minutes.	Very dry, brittle
Beets	Use only small, tender beets	Cook as usual; then cool, peel, and cut into shoestring strips ⅛" thick. No further blanching required.	Tough, leathery
Broccoli	Use young, fresh stalks	Trim and cut as for serving. Wash thoroughly. Quarter stalks lengthwise. *Blanch* (as directed on page 113), with steam 5 minutes or in water 4½ minutes.	Brittle
Brussels sprouts	Use small, tight, fresh sprouts	Cut in half lengthwise through stem. *Blanch* (as directed on page 113), with steam 6–7 minutes or in water 4½–5½ minutes.	Very dry to brittle
Cabbage	Copenhagen Market, Danish Ball Head, Golden Acre, Savoy Winningstradt	Remove outer leaves, then quarter and core. Cut into strips ⅛" thick. *Blanch* (as directed on page 113), with steam for 2½–3 minutes or in water for 1½–2 minutes.	Tough to brittle
Carrots	Danvers Half Long, Imperator, Morse, Bunching, Nantes (Chantenay not recommended). Use only crisp, tender carrots	Wash thoroughly. Cut off roots and tops; peel, if desired; cut in slices or strips ⅛" thick. *Blanch* (as directed on page 113), with steam for 6–7 minutes or in water 5–6 minutes.	Tough, leathery
Cauliflower		Break into small flowerettes. *Blanch* (as directed on page 113), with steam for 4–5 minutes or in water for 3–4 minutes.	Tough to brittle
Celery Both leaves and stalks may be dried	Use only crisp, tender stalks relatively free from "strings"; use small, green leaves	Trim stalks. Wash stalks and leaves thoroughly. Slice stalks. *Blanch* (as directed on page 113), with steam for 3–4 minutes or in water for 2–3 minutes.	Brittle
Corn on the cob	Stowells Evergreen, Country Gentlemen, Golden Bantam Ears should be young, tender, and in milk stage	Husk, trim. *Blanch,* with steam until milk does not exude from kernel when cut, usually 5–6 minutes, or in water 4–5 minutes.	Dry, brittle
Corn, cut	Use same varieties	Prepare same as corn on the cob, except cut corn from cob after blanching.	
Eggplant		Wash, trim, cut into ¼" slices. *Blanch* (as directed on page 113), with steam for 4 minutes or in water 3 minutes.	Brittle

(Continued on next page)

Vegetable	Best for drying	How to prepare	Test for dryness (Cool a piece before testing)
Horseradish		Wash; remove all small rootlets and stubs. Peel or scrape roots. Grate. No blanching needed.	Very dry and powdery
Mushrooms	Young, medium size, freshly gathered. "Gills" pink, free of insects or any blackening	Scrub thoroughly. Discard any tough, woody stalks. Cut tender stalks into short sections. Do not peel small mushrooms or "buttons." Peel large mushrooms and slice. *Blanch* (as directed on page 113), with steam for 3–4 minutes or in water 3 minutes.	Very dry and leathery
Okra		Wash, trim, and slice crosswise in ¼" to ⅛" strips. *Blanch* (as directed on page 113), with steam for 4–5 minutes or in water 3–4 minutes.	Tough to brittle
Onions	Ebenezer, Southport Globes, Sweet Spanish, White Portugal Use only onions with strong aroma and flavor	Wash and remove outer "paper shells." Remove tops and root ends and slice ⅛" to ¼" thick. No blanching needed.	Brittle
Parsley		Wash thoroughly. Separate clusters. Discard long or tough stems. No blanching needed.	Brittle, flaky
Peas	Use young, tender peas of a sweet variety (mature peas become tough and mealy)	Shell. *Blanch* (as directed on page 113), with steam for 3 minutes or in water 2 minutes.	Crisp, wrinkled
Peppers, bell	Green or red: California Wonder, Merrimack Wonder, Oakview Wonder	Wash; remove stem, seeds, partitions. Cut into ½"-square pieces. No blanching needed.	Brittle
Potatoes	Russett Burbank, White Rose	Wash, peel. Cut into shoestring strips ¼" thick, or cut in slices ⅛" thick. *Blanch* (as directed on page 113), with steam for 6–8 minutes or in water 5–6 minutes.	Brittle
Spinach and other greens (kale, chard, mustard)	Use only young, tender leaves	Trim, wash very thoroughly. *Blanch* (as directed on page 113), with steam for 2–3 minutes or in water 2 minutes.	Brittle
Squash, summer	Crookneck, pattypan, zucchini	Wash, trim, cut into ¼" slices. *Blanch* with steam for 3½–4 minutes or in water 3 minutes.	Brittle
Squash, winter	Banana	Wash, peel, slice in strips about ¼" thick. *Blanch* (as directed on page 113), with steam for 3 minutes or in water for 2 minutes.	Tough to brittle
	Hubbard	Cut or break into pieces. Remove seeds and seed cavity pulp. Cut into 1"-wide strips. Peel rind. Cut strips crosswise into pieces about ⅛" thick. *To blanch*, steam until tender.	Tough to brittle
Tomatoes	Firm ripe tomatoes with good color, no green spots	Dip in boiling water, then in cold water, and peel. Cut into sections about ¾" wide, or slice. Cut small pear or plum tomatoes in half. *Blanch* (as directed on page 113), with steam for 2–3 minutes or in water 1–2 minutes.	Slightly leathery

SMOKE-COOKING

The tantalizing flavor and rich mahogany color of smoke-cooked meat tempt many an outdoor cook to try smoke-cooking.

We've seen many smoking techniques as well as a host of "smoke ovens" or "smoke houses"—everything from discarded refrigerators and freezers to metal garbage cans. While there may be some merit to this kind of equipment, we found the easiest, most efficient way to smoke cook was in a covered barbecue.

Our versatile technique—smoking first with hickory chips in a covered barbecue, then oven roasting—is equally successful for beef, pork, turkey, and chicken. The trick is to maintain a consistently low temperature in your barbecue by using just a few hot coals at a time and using an oven thermometer to check the temperature frequently. Hot coals and presoaked hickory chips are then added at regular intervals throughout the 4 to 5-hour smoking period to maintain the low temperature.

Plan to do the smoking at least a day before you want to serve the meat. If you want cold meat for slicing, smoke, roast, and chill it well ahead. It will keep, refrigerated, for up to a week. If you want to serve it hot, do the smoking ahead of time, then finish roasting before serving.

Step-by-step smoke-cooking of meat & poultry

1 You'll need a covered barbecue with a tight-fitting lid or dome high enough to enclose the meat you plan to smoke. Have ready 16 to 20 whole long-burning briquets, 1 to 1½ pounds hickory or other hardwood chips, a small barbecue or old shallow metal pan for holding extra hot coals, an accurate oven or meat thermometer, and long-handled tongs for lifting hot coals.

2 On the lower rack of the barbecue, mound and ignite 12 briquets. When briquets are completely covered with gray ash, push 4 coals to each side of the lower rack, as far over as possible. Open top and bottom dampers.

3 Place remaining 4 hot coals in separate barbecue or pan; add several unignited coals so you will have a continuous supply of extra hot coals. (For each hot coal you add to your barbecue during smoking, add an unignited one to small barbecue to keep up your supply.)

4 Place 3 to 4 cups hickory chips in a bowl of water to soak for 20 minutes. (Every time you add hickory chips to the fire, add more hickory chips to water to keep up the supply.)

5 Between hot coals, center a foil drip pan. Grease cooking grill lightly and rotate it so you have access to heating coals. Place meat on grill (be sure no part of meat extends over coals); place thermometer beside or on top of meat near center of cooking grill.

6 Scoop out two handfuls of soaked chips; let drain briefly, then sprinkle one handful over each group of burning coals at sides of drip pan (use a long skewer to spread evenly). Cover barbecue, leaving top and bottom dampers open.

7 Check thermometer after 10 minutes. If temperature is below 140°F, add a hot coal to each side. If above 150°F, remove a coal from each side to lower temperature to 140° to 150°F. Continue to check thermometer every 30 to 40 minutes, adding or subtracting coals as needed to maintain 140° to 150°F. (You'll need to add about 1 coal each half-hour per side.) Also, when smoke is no longer coming out vents, add another handful of soaked, drained chips to each group of coals.

8 Meats and poultry will be smoked enough when they're golden brown (usually between 3 and 4½ hours). Lift meat off grill to a roasting pan. Remove drip pan; save drippings for gravy, if desired.

9 To serve meat hot, either oven roast it immediately or let it cool to room temperature, wrap in foil, and refrigerate up to 3 days; freeze for longer storage (see page 97). On the day you plan to serve the meat (defrost if frozen), finish roasting it in the oven. To serve meat cold, oven roast it right after smoking, then refrigerate until ready to use.

Meat, Poultry & Seafood Recipes

Smoked Roast Beef

A 3 to 5-pound rolled and tied boneless roast is ideal for smoke-cooking because it takes less time than a larger piece of meat.

3 to 5-pound boneless beef roast (such as sirloin tip or cross rib), rolled and tied
Briquets
Presoaked hickory chips

Follow steps 1–8, "Step-by-step smoke-cooking of meat and poultry," page 119. Remove from barbecue after 3 hours or when golden brown.

To complete cooking, insert a meat thermometer into thickest portion and roast in a 325° oven for 45 minutes (about 60 minutes, if refrigerated) or until meat thermometer registers 140°F for rare. Let stand for 15 minutes, then carve and serve hot. Or cool, cover, and refrigerate. Cut into thin slices and serve cold.

Smoked Pork Roast

An unusually good-tasting way to serve pork is to smoke cook it and serve it cold. You'll be surprised how moist the meat stays.

3 to 6-pound bone-in or boneless pork loin roast, rolled and tied
Briquets
Presoaked hickory chips

Follow steps 1–8, "Step-by-step smoke-cooking of meat and poultry," page 119. Remove from barbecue after 3 hours or when golden brown.

To complete cooking, insert a meat thermometer into thickest portion and roast in a 325° oven for 1 to 1½ hours (1½ to 2 hours, if refrigerated) or until thermometer registers 170°F. Let stand for 15 minutes, then carve and serve hot. Or cool, cover, and refrigerate. Cut into slices and serve cold.

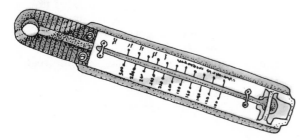

Savory Smoked Turkey

You'll never taste a better bird than this mouth-watering, moist turkey. It's an excellent way to get the cook out of the kitchen during the holidays; you can smoke-cook the family turkey up to 3 days before Thanksgiving, then finish roasting it on the holiday afternoon for an early dinner.

15 to 20-pound turkey, thawed if frozen
Briquets
Presoaked hickory chips
Poultry stuffing (optional)
Basting sauce or melted butter (optional)

Remove neck and giblets from turkey and reserve for other uses. Rinse turkey inside and out; pat dry. Fasten neck skin to back with skewers. Tie wings to body or tuck them in back of bird, akimbo-style; leave legs untied.

Follow steps 1–8, "Step-by-step smoke-cooking of meat and poultry," page 119. Remove from barbecue after 4 to 4½ hours or when golden brown.

If turkey is to be served hot, you may want to stuff it; do this after bird has been smoked and just before basting. Remove skewers and lightly fill neck cavity with stuffing; again fasten neck skin to back with skewers. Then lightly stuff body cavity; fit a piece of foil over cavity opening. (Do *not* stuff turkey if you plan to serve it cold.)

Place bird, breast side down, on a rack in a shallow roasting pan. Insert meat thermometer into thickest portion of thigh (make sure it doesn't touch bone). Brush with basting sauce or melted butter, if desired; cover loosely with foil.

Roast in a 325° oven, basting occasionally, for 2 to 2½ hours (3½ to 4 hours, if refrigerated) or until meat thermometer registers 180° to 185°F. Let stand for 20 to 30 minutes before carving; serve hot. Or cool, wrap in foil, and refrigerate and serve cold.

Smoke-Cooked Whole Chicken

Maybe you've never thought of smoking a chicken before, but next time you're planning an outdoor party or need something special to carry along to a picnic, try smoke-cooking one or more chickens.

3 to 5-pound whole broiler-fryer or roasting chicken
Briquets
Presoaked hickory chips

(Continued on page 122)

DRYING IN A CONVECTION OVEN

If you can bear to give your convection oven a break from baking, why not use it to dehydrate irresistible seasonal buys of fruit?

Read the information on page 102 about selecting fruit and about why some fruits discolor. Check the chart below to see which fruits need to be pretreated with an antidarkening agent. Pretreat with a commercial powdered fruit preservative or by soaking cut fruit in a solution of ascorbic acid and water for about an hour.

Fruit dehydrates most effectively when the convection oven is set at 140° to 150°F and the oven door is left ajar about a half-inch. We suggest you rotate trays every few hours so that fruit dries evenly. Cool a piece of fruit to test for doneness—it should be pliable and leathery.

For packaging instructions, follow steps 6 and 7 of "Step-by-step directions for sun drying fruit" on page 105.

The chart below is a general guide. The length of time it takes to dehydrate fruit varies, depending on its size and moisture content, the humidity of the air, and the oven temperature used.

Fruit	Best for drying	How to prepare	Drying time	Test for dryness (Cool a piece before testing)
Apples	Firm varieties: Yellow Newtown Pippin, Gravenstein, Rome Beauty, Jonathan	Peel, cut off ends, core and cut into ⅛"-thick rings. Pretreat with antidarkening agent.	5–8 hours	Soft, leathery, pliable
Apricots	Blenheim (Royal), Tilton	Wash, cut in half, remove pits. Pretreat with antidarkening agent.	18–24 hours	Soft, pliable, slightly moist in center when cut
Bananas	Firm varieties	Peel, cut into ⅛"-thick slices. Pretreat with antidarkening agent.	20–24 hours	Leathery and pliable
Figs	Black Mission, Kadota	(Leave figs on tree; when fully ripe they drop to the ground.) Wash, cut in half or leave whole.	24–36 hours	Leathery outside but still pliable, slightly sticky inside.
Grapes	Thompson Seedless, Muscat	Wash, leave whole. Leave stems on until after drying.	16–24 hours	Raisinlike texture, wrinkled
Nectarines and Peaches	Freestone varieties	Wash, cut in half, remove pits. Peeling is optional. Pretreat with antidarkening agent.	24–36 hours	Soft, pliable, slightly moist in center
Pears	Bartlett	Wash, peel, cut in half, core. Pretreat with antidarkening agent.	24–36 hours	Soft, pliable, slightly moist in center
Persimmons	Firm varieties	Wash, cut into ½"-thick rings.	8–24 hours	Leathery

Remove neck and giblets from chicken and reserve for other uses. Rinse chicken inside and out; pat dry. Fasten neck skin to back with skewers. Tie wings to body or tuck them in back, akimbo-style; leave legs untied.

Follow steps 1–8, "Step-by-step smoke-cooking of meat and poultry," page 119. Remove from barbecue after 1½ to 2 hours or when golden brown.

To complete cooking, roast in a 325° oven for about 30 minutes (60 minutes, if refrigerated) or until juices run clear. Let stand for 15 minutes, then carve and serve hot. Or cool, cover, and refrigerate; cut into pieces and serve cold.

Smoked-Cooked Salmon
(Pictured on page 111)

An impressive entrée or an equally pleasing hors d'oeuvre, this popular version of smoked salmon is bound to draw raves from your guests. Have your fishmonger clean the fish, cut off the head and tail, and cut the fish lengthwise into two boneless fillets, leaving the skin on. Use tweezers to pull out all remaining small bones.

> Syrup baste (recipe follows)
> 7 to 8-pound whole salmon, cleaned and filleted
> Salt brine (recipe follows)
> Briquets
> Presoaked hickory chips

Prepare syrup baste; set aside. Arrange fillets in a shallow pan. Prepare salt brine and pour over fish. Cover and let stand at room temperature for 2 to 3 hours or refrigerate for up to 6 hours. Drain fish, rinse in cold water, and pat dry.

Place fillets, skin side down, on several thicknesses of paper towels and let stand at room temperature for 30 minutes. Arrange fillets, skin side down, on a double thickness of cheesecloth, and cut cheesecloth to outline of fish. Leave cheesecloth under fillets when you lift it and transfer it to grill.

Follow steps 1–7, "Step-by-step smoke-cooking of meat and poultry," page 119. During cooking period, occasionally use a paper towel to dab away any white juices that ooze from fish, then brush with syrup baste. Smoke-cook salmon for 2½ to 3 hours or until fish flakes readily when prodded in thickest portion with a fork.

Gently slide fillets onto flat cooky sheets and let cool 30 minutes at room temperature; then cover and refrigerate for up to 2 weeks. For longer storage, wrap fish securely in freezer wrap and freeze.

To serve, transfer cold (thawed, if frozen) fillets to a large serving board. Makes 5 pounds smoked salmon (about 50 appetizer servings).

Syrup baste. Stir together 4 tablespoons **maple-flavored syrup**, 2 tablespoons **soy sauce**, ¼ teaspoon *each* **ground ginger** and **pepper**, and 1 clove **garlic**, minced or pressed.

Salt brine. In 2 quarts water, dissolve 1 cup **salt** and 1½ cups **sugar**; add 3 tablespoons coarse ground **pepper** and 3 **bay leaves**.

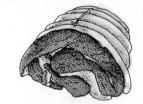

HOW TO MAKE MEAT JERKY

To survive the grueling trek across the Sierra Nevada, Jedediah Smith and other "mountain men" often relied on leathery morsels of sun-dried meat they had carefully stored in their saddlebags days before.

Beef jerky is still a staple in the packs of today's mountain men—backpackers, skiers, and campers—and a popular snack for armchair sports, too.

You can dry meat in the sun, but oven drying is the simplest way to make jerky. Start with thin, seasoned strips of meat.

You can also dry fully cooked ham. Because you start with smoked meat, ham jerky requires no additional seasoning from a marinade. Serve it as a snack to nibblers or crumble it as you would bits of bacon to flavor or garnish other dishes. (If the ham is quite salty, eating the ham jerky on a hike may make you thirsty.)

Partially freezing any meat before cutting makes it easier to slice evenly. Cut with the grain of the meat if you like a chewy jerky; cut across the grain for a more tender, brittle product. We offer five recipes for delicious, old-fashioned jerky—three made in the oven and two dried in the sun.

Jerky Recipes

Oven Dried Jerky

The following recipe is for lean cuts of beef (flank, brisket, or round steak), venison, and the white meat of turkey or chicken.

1½ to 2 pounds lean, boneless meat (see above), partially frozen
¼ cup soy sauce
1 tablespoon Worcestershire
¼ teaspoon *each* pepper and garlic powder
½ teaspoon onion powder
1 teaspoon hickory smoke-flavored salt

Trim and discard all fat and connective tissue from meat. Cut into ⅛ to ¼-inch-thick slices (with or across the grain, as desired). If necessary, cut large slices to make strips about 1½ inches wide and as long as possible.

In a bowl, combine soy, Worcestershire, pepper, garlic powder, onion powder, and smoke-flavored salt. Stir until seasonings are dissolved. Add meat strips and mix until all surfaces are thoroughly coated. (Meat will absorb most of the liquid.) Cover and let stand for 1 hour or refrigerate until next day.

Shaking off any excess liquid, arrange strips of meat close together but not overlapping, directly on oven racks or on cake racks set in shallow, rimmed baking pans.

Dry meat at 150° to 200°F until it has turned brown, feels hard, and is dry to the touch (about 5 hours for chicken and turkey, 4 to 7 hours for beef and venison). Pat off any beads of oil. Let cool, then remove from racks and store in airtight containers or plastic bags.

Store at cool room temperature or in the refrigerator until ready to use; it keeps indefinitely. Makes about ½ pound.

Oven Dried Ham Jerky

Here's a tasty version that's bound to please any jerky fan. Start with leftover ham or have your butcher slice fully cooked ham about ¼ inch thick.

1½ to 2 pounds fully cooked boneless ham, cut ¼ inch thick

Trim and discard all fat from ham. Cut slices to make strips as long as possible. Arrange strips close together but not overlapping, directly on oven racks or on cake racks set in shallow, rimmed baking pans.

Dry ham at 150° to 200°F for 5 to 6 hours or until it feels hard and snaps readily. Pat off any beads of oil. Let cool, then remove from racks and store in airtight containers or plastic bags. Store at cool room temperature or in the refrigerator. Makes about ½ pound.

Chinese Beef Jerky

Chinese jerky typically is moister and less brittle than cowboy jerky. The reason for this difference lies in the way Chinese jerky is prepared. The meat is cooked first in two stages, eliminating the extensive drying that most uncooked jerky requires.

First you cut the meat into large chunks and simmer it in a sweetly spiced soy mixture for a short time, then cool and chill it. This initial cooking makes it easier to slice the meat thinly and also helps prevent the pieces from curling up. After slicing, you return the meat to the liquid and cook it until all the liquid is absorbed.

After this precooking, drying the meat in a moderately hot oven for a short time preserves it enough so you can keep it moist and tender for several months in the refrigerator.

The cooking liquid is an aromatic, cinnamon-flavored sauce with a hint of soy and hot chilies or curry powder.

3 pounds lean boneless beef (such as rump or sirloin tip), cut into strips about 3 inches thick and wide
2 cups water
⅓ cup soy sauce
1 tablespoon red wine or dry Sherry
¼ cup sugar
1 teaspoon salt
2 whole star anise or equivalent broken pieces (or omit anise and use 5 whole allspice and ¾ teaspoon anise seed)
5 thin slices of fresh ginger (*each* about 1 inch in diameter)
2 green onions
3 or 4 small dried hot chili peppers (optional) or 1 tablespoon curry powder (optional)

Trim off excess fat from meat.

In a 12-inch frying pan, combine water, soy, red wine, sugar, salt, whole anise, ginger, green onions, and chili peppers or curry powder, if desired.

(Continued on next page)

Bring mixture to a boil, then add meat; cover and simmer, turning meat occasionally, until firm, 20 to 30 minutes. Remove from cooking liquid, cool, and chill at least 1 hour or until cool and firm. Reserve cooking liquid.

Thinly slice cold meat across the grain; return meat to cooking liquid. Cook, uncovered, over medium heat, turning pieces occasionally, for 40 to 50 minutes or until all liquid is absorbed (lower the heat and turn meat more frequently as liquid is absorbed). Discard onions, ginger, and whole spices.

For moist-style beef jerky, arrange strips of meat slightly apart in a single layer on cooky sheets. Bake, uncovered, in a 300° oven (with door slightly ajar) for 20 to 25 minutes or until dry to the touch but still pliable. Pat any beads of oil off with paper towels. Let cool thoroughly; store airtight in plastic bags or containers, for up to 2 months in the refrigerator or for a few days at cool room temperature.

For drier jerky, arrange stips of meat close together but not overlapping on oven racks or on cake racks set in shallow rimmed baking pans. Bake at lowest possible oven temperature (140° to 180°F) for 3 to 5 hours or until dry to the touch but still pliable. Pat any beads of oil off with paper towels. Let cool thoroughly; store in airtight containers or plastic bags in the refrigerator for up to 6 months or at cool room temperature for 1 week. Makes 1 pound jerky.

Texas-style Jerky

This slightly hot-flavored jerky can be made outdoors in the sun or in the oven. It starts with lean top round steak, thinly sliced.

1 **pound very lean top round steak**
4 **teaspoons salt**
1 **teaspoon** *each* **pepper, chili powder, garlic powder, and onion powder**
¼ **teaspoon cayenne**
3 **dashes liquid smoke**
½ **cup water**

Trim meat carefully, removing any fat or connective tissue, and place in the freezer to partially freeze (about 1 hour). While meat is in freezer, combine salt, pepper, chili powder, garlic powder, onion powder, cayenne, and liquid smoke in a bowl. Pour in water, stirring to blend well.

When meat is firm enough, cut across the grain in thin, slanting slices about ⅛ inch thick. Place slices in the marinade, stir, cover, and chill several hours or until next day, stirring occasionally.

Remove strips from marinade, drain, and spread on cake racks placed on baking sheets. Expose to hot sun until thoroughly dry but still somewhat pliable (6 to 7 hours). Arrange cheesecloth over strips while they are drying to protect from insects.

For oven drying, arrange meat on racks the same way you would for sun drying and place in a 150° to 200° oven with door slightly ajar. Dry until a test piece cracks but does not break in two when bent (about 6 hours).

Let cool, remove from racks, and store airtight in plastic bags at room temperature for up to 3 days or in refrigerator for up to 2 weeks. Makes about ½ pound jerky.

Sun Dried Jerky

This jerky "cooks" in the sun all afternoon and comes out quite spicy because of all the goodies in the marinade. For those living under cloudy skies, there are directions at the end of the recipe for oven drying.

1 **pound lean top round steak, partially frozen**
2 **tablespoons salad oil**
⅓ **cup soy sauce**
2 **tablespoons firmly packed brown sugar**
1 **tablespoon sherry**
1 **clove garlic, minced or pressed**
¼ **teaspoon ground ginger**

Trim and discard all fat and connective tissue from meat. Cut diagonally across the grain into ⅛ to ¼-inch-thick slices.

In a bowl, combine oil, soy, sugar, sherry, garlic, and ginger. Stir well to blend. Place strips of meat in marinade and stir. Cover and refrigerate for several hours or until next day, stirring occasionally.

Remove strips from marinade, drain, and spread on cake racks placed on baking sheets. Expose to hot sun until thoroughly dry but still somewhat pliable (6 to 7 hours). Arrange cheesecloth over strips while they are drying to protect from insects, and either cover strips or bring them inside at night. Let cool, remove from racks, and store in airtight containers or plastic bags. Store at cool room temperature or in the refrigerator. Makes about ½ pound.

For oven drying, arrange meat on racks as for sun drying above and place in a 150° to 200°F oven with the door slightly ajar. Dry until a test piece cracks but does not break in two when you bend it (about 6 hours).

DRYING FRESH HERBS

(Pictured on page 98)

If you have an abundance of fresh herbs on hand in summer, you may want to preserve some for later use. For our photo, we selected sage, basil, marjoram, rosemary, and thyme.

Drying is the easiest method of preserving herbs. You simply expose the leaves, flowers, or seeds to warm, dry air until the moisture is gone. The best time to harvest most herbs for drying is when the flowers first open.

Bunch drying is an easy method to use for herbs with long stems, such as marjoram, sage, savory, mint, parsley, and rosemary. Cut long branches and rinse in cool water, discarding any leaves that are dead or have lost their color. Tie the ends of the stems together into small bunches and hang them upside down in a warm, dry room (or outdoors) where they won't be exposed to direct sunlight.

A warm, even temperature from 70° to 90°F is best. Air should circulate freely around the drying herbs to remove their moisture, so don't hang them against a wall. (Note that our photo shows bunches of *previously dried* herbs used to decorate a wall.) If you dry herbs outdoors, bring them in at night so the dew won't dampen them.

To avoid collecting dust on the drying herbs, place each bunch inside a paper bag, gathering the top and tying the stem ends so that the herb leaves hang freely inside the bag. Cut out the bottom of the bag or punch air holes in the sides for ventilation.

After a week or two, the herbs should be crackling dry. Carefully remove the leaves without breaking them; they retain flavor longer if left whole until ready to use; then store in sealed containers.

Tray drying is best for seeds, large-leafed herbs, and short-tipped stems that are difficult to tie together for hanging. Screens or trays can be made to any size; use window screening or cheesecloth for the drying deck. Rinse the herbs, shaking off excess moisture.

To dry leaves, you can either remove them from their stems or leave them attached, but spread only one layer of leaves on each tray. If you attempt to dry too many at once, air will not reach them evenly, and they'll take longer to cure. Put the trays in a warm, dry room in a place where air can circulate freely around them.

Every few days, stir or turn the leaves gently to assure even, thorough drying. It should take a week or so for them to dry completely, depending on the temperature and humidity. When leaves are crisp and thoroughly dry, take them off the racks.

Seeds can be spread on the trays or screens in a thin layer and dried in the same way as leaves. Once they're dry, carefully rub the seed capsules through your hands, gently blowing away chaff.

Microwave ovens offer faster drying of herbs. Rinse the herbs as for bunch or tray drying, shaking off excess moisture (if you put wet herbs in a microwave oven, they'll cook instead of dry). Put no more than four or five herb branches in the oven between two paper towels. Turn oven on high for 2 to 3 minutes; remove from oven and place herbs on a rack. If they're not brittle and dry when removed from the oven, repeat the microwave drying for 30 seconds more. Then store as for regular dried herbs.

Convection ovens provide a new, easy way to dry herbs, though there is some flavor loss at higher temperatures. Use an oven setting as low as possible (about 120°F) and leave the oven door ajar about ½ inch. Prepare herbs as for bunch or tray drying. Herbs dry quickly, so you should check them after the first 45 minutes. Most take between 1 and 3 hours; test for doneness by rubbing a few herbs to see if they crumble readily. Store as for regular dried herbs.

INDEX

Metric Conversion Table

To change	To	Multiply by
ounces (oz.)	grams (g)	28
pounds (lbs.)	kilograms (kg)	0.45
teaspoons	milliliters (ml)	5
tablespoons	milliliters (ml)	15
fluid ounces (fl. oz.)	milliliters (ml)	30
cups	liters (l)	0.24
pints (pt.)	liters (l)	0.47
quarts (qt.)	liters (l)	0.95
gallons (gal.)	liters (l)	3.8
Fahrenheit temperature (°F)	Celsius temperature (°C)	5/9 after subtracting 32